Robin reaches the reader by combining the language of an addict with the healing power of the Spirit. She connects by using the "Me too's" of anyone struggling with alcohol, drugs, or addiction of any type; and finds God's response through Scripture, personal experience, and what surely must be countless prayers. As a former addict and very present child of God, I loved it!

—JOHAN UGGLA
PASTOR, TUESDAY OUTREACH MINISTRIES
EAST POINT, GEORGIA

It has been my pleasure to see Robin Cantwell's faith and humility first hand. Robin's new book is an open and frank discussion of what God has shown her as she wins one of our most common battles. If you are one of the many that struggles with a life-draining addiction, I know you will find this book helpful and inspiring.

—STEVE CRAIG
PASTOR, HIS HANDS CHURCH
WOODSTOCK, GEORGIA

ADDICTIONS SUCK

ADDICTIONS SUCK

ROBIN D. CANTWELL

CREATION
HOUSE
A STRANG COMPANY

Design Director: Bill Johnson
Cover design by Amanda Potter

Library of Congress Control Number: 2009927899
International Standard Book Number: 978-1-59979-778-6

First Edition

09 10 11 12 13 — 987654321
Printed in the United States of America

I dedicate this book to any and everyone who has, is, or will ever struggle with addiction in any form. There is hope for a new and better life.

ACKNOWLEDGMENTS

FIRST AND FOREMOST I HAVE TO THANK JESUS CHRIST, my Lord and Savior. Apart from Him I would be physically, spiritually, and mentally dead. He has never given up on me or stopped loving me, even though I have given Him every reason to.

To the lady I refer to as my tech support, Jennifer Waters. Without her, this book wouldn't have been written, as she had to teach me almost everything I know about using a computer. She was always available and had to bail me out on many occasions. Thanks, girlie.

To my number one sister, DeeAnn McCormick, who was available for whatever I needed in order to make this book happen.

I must thank my new best friend, Johan Uggla, who prayed for and with me countless times, gave me information and inspiration for the content, and encouraged me when I wanted to give up.

To all my friends and family I didn't mention, thank you for your prayers, love, and support and for not telling me I was crazy for taking on such a huge project.

CONTENTS

Chapter 1

ADDICTIONS SUCK

This is a trustworthy saying, and everyone should accept it: "Christ Jesus came into the world to save sinners"—and I am the worst of them all. But God had mercy on me so that Christ Jesus could use me as a prime example of his great patience with even the worst sinners. Then others will realize that they, too, can believe in him and receive eternal life. All honor and glory to God forever and ever! He is the eternal King, the unseen one who never dies; he alone is God. Amen.
—1 TIMOTHY 1:15–17

I THINK THE ABOVE SCRIPTURE IS AN EXCELLENT portrayal of who I was and at times feel I still am. I have been addicted to almost everything there is to be addicted to: sexual immorality (many forms); drugs, including cigarettes; alcohol; money; food; and mental strongholds, such as pride, being critical, lying, judging, worrying, fearfulness, and negativity.

I have written this book to help any and everyone who

is or has ever been affected by addictions or who is in a relationship with someone consumed by addictions. My hope and prayer is that you will find hope, freedom, encouragement, and peace as you make your journey into the promised land of freedom; freedom not just from addictions of any kind, but also from the guilt, shame, and condemnation that so often, if not always, accompanies them.

If you are like me, you may struggle with many types of addictions. Don't think that you will see deliverance from them all at once, even though "with God all things are possible" (Matt. 19:26, NKJV). In my experience, our progress is gradual, somewhat painful and difficult, different for everyone and from how we perceive it to be, but it *is* worth the trip. Will you please join me on this exciting journey into the promised land of freedom? Put on your seat belt, settle down, and get ready for a life-changing adventure. I guarantee you that it will be worth the ride, regardless of how many times you may get sidetracked, lost, or even blindsided along the way.

Addictions drain our time, money, mental energies, health, and self-confidence. Depending on the addiction, they can draw any and all of these things from us and our loved ones. Think about it. Let's say your addiction is smoking cigarettes or drugs. You have to plan on when and where you will smoke, therefore depleting your time by planning and going to the location of choice. You have to spend your time going to the store or dealer, making the call, and setting up the time to go buy the substance and paraphernalia that goes with it. You have invested your time, your money, and your strength and have neglected something and someone in the process.

Maybe your addiction is food. Your time is spent thinking about what to eat, where to go to eat, how to prepare it, how much you can eat, and whether or not you need to sneak in order to eat all you want. After you have gorged yourself, it then saps your physical energy because you're stuffed. Your mental energy is wasted on feelings of guilt and disgust over how obese you are, which then leads to more binging. Maybe you're not even fat because you purge or are anorexic; either way, your mind or body is consumed with the addiction.

Let's say your addiction is sex. Your mental state is consumed with thoughts of sex or how and when you can sneak away to a computer or magazine or to a hooker or your next lover to satisfy the burning desire you feel whenever the thought crosses your mind. It robs your time, your privacy, and your self-respect.

If your addiction is gambling or shopping, then your money is siphoned away on spending for what you don't need or gambling away what little you do have left. When you don't have the money to spend or gamble away, then your time is consumed thinking about how you can get the money. Sometimes this is by legal means and sometimes not.

In my opinion, an addiction is anything that absorbs your time, money, and energy. This happens by either actually engaging in the addiction or by preparing for it. It is the one thing you turn to when things get tough. It's what you want to do with your free time and what you wish you could be doing when you're busy with life. Even things like work are done so you will have a means of supporting your addiction. It affects every area of your life, whether you admit it or not.

Why am I going into the obvious? Because although we know these things in the back of our minds, we have pushed them back there so we don't have to deal with the truth of our choices. If we ignore the consequences, we can continue in the behavior while still secretly hating the addiction thereby causing more reasons to self-medicate. Does any of this sound familiar? We need to face the truth about where we are right now.

Let's say you don't have any addictions but you are in a relationship with someone who does. I know from experience that we can become addicted to the person who is addicted by allowing their choices to control us. The counseling world calls it being co-dependent. This too drains us because the bad choices of other people do inadvertently affect us. This can cause us to feel hopeless and helpless. The sad truth is that to some extent, we are.

There is hope and help but unfortunately we are helpless to change the addicted person. Regardless of how bad they need to and should change, we can't make it happen. There is nothing we have done to make them have this addiction; it is their choice. And there is also nothing we can do to make them stop their addiction. By nothing, I mean that our actions in and of themselves won't change a person. The one action that will effect change is to pray for that person and love and forgive that person, regardless of their actions. You can pray for yourself not to be pulled into their bad choices by being controlled by them or somehow enabling them to continue. The feeling of rejection is very strong but we can receive healing for ourselves apart from the addicted person. There is more on this in the chapter "Let Me Help You."

Maybe you are thinking that you don't have any addictions. Have you considered the many mental addictions? Think about pride, judgment, perfectionism, gossip, guilt, blame, or even fear. I do believe that fear is a spirit and a mental stronghold, but it can also be classified as an addiction because it is a state of mind to which we are in the habit of turning. Just because we think we have no control over these things doesn't mean that is the truth or reality. The truth is that Jesus made a way for us to have an abundant life, a life of freedom, joy, peace, and self-control.

> The thief does not come except to steal, and to kill, and to destroy. I have come that they may have life, and that they may have it more abundantly.
>
> —JOHN 10:9–11, NKJV

Mental addictions are harder to deal with because many times we are ignorant of them. The truth is that they are often apparent to others. Their fruit is evident through our attitudes and words spoken, even if we don't admit to having them. They are usually deep rooted and often hidden. My hope is that after you read this book, they will be identified and then crucified because "you will know the truth, and the truth will set you free" (John 8:32).

This book is about freedom and no longer living a life

that has been drained of life. People who are addicted hate their addiction. It's easy to hate an addiction as soon as the need is satisfied, whatever that need may be. For the drug addict, it's the toke or smoke or hit. The shopper swears off sales after spending another hundred dollars they don't have. The gambler will place that one last bet just knowing this will be the payoff that gets them through. The sex addict swears that's the last affair or bout with porn or whatever their preference for release is.

To move forward with the solution, we must first acknowledge there is an addiction and that it is distasteful and draining our very life from us. We are powerless to control it, so it controls us. We want to quit but keep being drawn to it, over and over and over again. Maybe there is guilt afterwards and sometimes even before or during, but the addiction stays. Sometimes we can even break free for a short time with much struggle; but then we return to it because we can't take the pressure of the struggle anymore. We find ourselves in a continuing cycle.

We must recognize and hate the sin enough to get to the place we are willing to go through the pain that will bring us to freedom. You can't break free from something you still love. Why would you? Maybe the first step is to pray and ask God to help you hate the sin as much as He does. And then ask Him to start showing you the freedom that comes without that sin in your life. Once you start to truly hate the sin, you can begin to desire real freedom, even at the cost of suffering. I heard Joyce Meyer say that you are suffering either way, but with an addiction it's an ongoing suffering with nothing but ever increasing trouble. On the other hand, with freedom, the suffering will end—without fail! That's the truth and reality of the situation.

Every person is different and there are many, many different addictions but the mental struggles are the same. The path to freedom is also the same. We must start by doing without the addictive substance, behavior, or thoughts, while facing the fact that we may suffer until we are free. Is it worth it? *Yes!* When we first set out on our journey of freedom, we will ask ourselves a hundred times a day if it's worth it; but the answer is always the same a hundred times a day: *Yes!*

You are in a battle and must decide that enough is enough. You are losing the battle more and more every day, and you eventually lose your life, causing casualties around you. The good news is that there is freedom from the pain and struggle, and it will come eventually. There is freedom from the pull and drive that comes with any addiction. The biggest obstacle is to not give up. You must desire that freedom more than you desire being in your self-inflicted prison.

Addictions, regardless of what they are, need not be our life-long companions or even our worst enemies. They can be the very tools used to bring us to the loving, saving knowledge of Jesus Christ. If you already have a personal relationship with Christ, these can be the tools used to bring you into a deeper understanding of His love, grace, and forgiveness. If you have no idea who Jesus is, just ask Him to show Himself to you. He will. Say: *Jesus, I want You to be my Leader and Forgiver. I believe You died for me to be free from my life of sin.*

This is how much God loved the world: He gave his Son, his one and only Son. And this is why: so that no one need be destroyed; by believing in him, anyone can have a whole and lasting life. God didn't go to all the trouble of sending his Son merely to point an accusing finger, telling the world how bad it was. He came to help, to put the world right again. Anyone who trusts in him is acquitted; anyone who refuses to trust him has long since been under the death sentence without knowing it. And why? Because of that person's failure to believe in the one-of-a-kind Son of God when introduced to him.

—JOHN 3:16–18, THE MESSAGE

I have been in many addictions throughout my lifetime, and I come from a family full of addicts. These addictions varied from drug abuse, drinking, cigarette smoking, sexual immorality, or gluttony, to gossip, being critical, being easily offended, pride, rage or anger, or judgment—to name just a few. So when I say addictions suck, I say it from firsthand experience and with authority. For most of my life, I have been in a family whose addictions affected me in a horribly negative way, or have been the one addicted bringing devastation to myself and others. Neither is a good place to be. With this type of background, I want to offer hope, understanding, and maybe even a fresh perspective to you as the addicted, or bring new insight towards a loved one suffering with addiction.

The good news is that no matter how bad the addiction is or how long you have contended with it in your life, there is hope of freedom. It is typical to fall back into the same behaviors you have successfully changed in the past so don't let that slip dishearten you.

My desire is not to give you a formula or a twelve step program on how to get out of your particular addiction but to encourage you to never give up on giving it up. This too shall pass. The wait, the suffering of doing without your wrong choice of temporary comfort, is all worth it to receive freedom. Don't let doubt and despair get you down or keep you down. No matter how many times you have given in or tried to quit and failed, remember that each day is a new day. With and without failures, each day we have is a learning experience, not a beat-yourself-up day.

> This is the day the LORD has made; let us rejoice
> and be glad in it.
>
> —PSALM 118:24, NKJV

I understand being stuck in addictions and the yoyo effect of thinking I want to be free but I don't know how to be. I want to quit but it's too hard. I want a quick fix but there isn't one. We want instant freedom, but apart from God there isn't any freedom.

> Anyone who separates from me is deadwood,
> gathered up and thrown on the bonfire. But if
> you make yourselves at home with me and my
> words are at home in you, you can be sure that

whatever you ask will be listened to and acted upon.

—JOHN 15:6–7, THE MESSAGE

What do we do when we ask for freedom from our addictions but the thoughts, feelings, and habits are still there? We just keep going without getting drawn away from the results. We must acknowledge God with our feelings and choices. We keep asking. We ask for patience as He works in our hearts and renews our minds with His words. We have allowed addictions to pull the life from us and our families long enough.

Today is your day, your day to live a new life. This is your day to change your thinking. This is your day to ask for a desire to walk in freedom. The fact that you are reading this book is proof that you haven't and won't give up. You are on the way to a new life in Christ Jesus.

> Therefore, if anyone is in Christ, he is a new creation; old things have passed away; behold, all things have become new.
>
> —2 CORINTHIANS 5:17, NKJV

Here is a prayer that came out of my desperate need for freedom and repentance. You may pray it, or pray however you feel led. I hope it helps.

Dear Lord,
Forgive me for I have sinned against You in my body and Spirit. I have done what I felt like doing

instead of trusting and obeying You. You know what's best for me even when I don't. You have a good plan for me, a future and a hope, not a plan for the evil I have committed against You. The wages of sin is death and I am being paid my salary. Let me quit this job of working at sin. Let me receive Your wages of forgiveness, mercy, truth, and grace. Teach me to wait upon You, especially while all I want to do is get, grab, and cling to earthly fleshly desires. I'm trying to meet my own needs in my own way and it is causing me great pain, worry, and frustration. My heart is broken. My pain is real. Hear and help me, O Lord, in Your way and in Your timing. Forgive me, O Lord, for my sins are many, too many to count. I've been greedy, chasing after fleshly lusts. I've lied and turned my back on You, my family, and friends because of my selfish desires, which don't satisfy. My mind has been consumed with things that are not of You. I so long for an immediate release, but I am grabbing any and everything but You to fill the void. I go to You, but I feel the pain more than I feel You. I know You are real, so help me, Lord. I confess my selfishness, Lord, that when I do come to You, it's been to use You for comfort. Help me, Lord Jesus. Do not turn from me in my time of despair, even though I deserve it. I deserve punishment, but I pray for mercy and Your loving-kindness. I desire Your will but my flesh (evil desires and tendencies) cry out loudly! Silence them with Your loving

touch and embrace. Quiet my unrest and dissat-
isfaction of where I am. You are loving and kind
and will withhold no good thing from me, help my
unbelief. When my flesh cries and screams like a
baby wanting its pacifier, help soothe and comfort
me with Your loving Father's arms. Rock me gently
and tell me of Your unfailing love for me. Show
me hope and strengthen me to keep going when
all I want to do is die to escape the crushing pain.
Sometimes it feels too overwhelming. Where is my
joy, peace, and trust? I have given them away to
another. I'm sorry, Lord. Have Your way in my
life, regardless of how much I fight You. Where
there is confusion, please bring clarity, even if I
have to ask a thousand times. I'm so glad You are
longsuffering. I feel as if I tire You with my many
petitions and lack of obedience, but You instruct
me to make my request known to You, so I will, yet
again. Thank You for hope. Thank You for loving
me in the midst of my trouble and despair. Thank
You for teaching me that the earthly things I crave
only bring heartache. You alone satisfy. Help me
to believe that with my whole being. Thank You for
not giving up on me. Thank You for dying for me to
be free. Enable me to die to my wants and desires,
to know the Truth that I may be free. I choose this
day to wait on you, no matter how much it hurts
and no matter how much I don't understand. You
will lift me up. You, O Lord, will cause me to be
victorious for Your name's sake. You will have

mercy on me because You are merciful. Though I walk through the valley of the shadow of death, I will fear no evil. Your rod and your staff, they comfort me. Surely mercy and goodness will follow me all the days of my life. I am Yours, O Lord. Be gentle with me as I am hurt and bruised because of my own doings. Restore me and make me what You desire me to be, which is whole, complete, and useful for good works. Thank You, O Lord, my God and my Redeemer.

In Jesus' name I pray. Amen.

Chapter 2

QUIT STRUGGLING WITH YOUR STRUGGLES

I WANT TO SHARE WITH YOU SOME OF THE THOUGHTS and feelings I have had during my times of walking out addictions. The purpose of my sharing is so that you can see that you are not alone and someone else can relate to your feelings. Hopefully you will also know that it is possible to make it through and that the same lies you are hearing have been heard by someone else. The same truth can also be used and believed to bring freedom.

One of the many lies I have heard in my head and believed was that doing without my addiction was going to kill me; in other words, I would die or explode if I had to be straight or do without a cigarette. I really thought at times that my head or body would explode from the pressure and pain I was feeling. The good news is that I am sitting here in one piece typing, which means I didn't shatter into a million pieces like I felt I would. No matter how intense our feelings are, we must remember that they are not the rulers of our lives, our mind is. We must input the truth of God's Word into our mind and let that lead us.

Another one of the lies we will face and have to conquer is that it is easier to just give in. We think that we can't do this again so we might as well just give in and end the pain and suffering. By giving in, we just perpetuate the pain and struggle. The truth is that if we want that pain and struggle to end, we must do without our fix. We must surrender to the temporary pain of withdrawal so that we may receive a lifetime of freedom.

A good comparison would be that of a visit to the dentist. Who likes going to the dentist to have a toothache fixed? Probably no one; but we know if we want the pain to go away, we must endure a little suffering so that the pain will cease. We can choose not to go to the dentist and endure our pain or choose to accept the worsening toothache pain in hopes it will go away. We all know that until we deal with that toothache in a productive manner, it will not go away but will get worse with each passing day.

An addiction is just like that. With each passing day of giving it permission to stay in our lives, we are allowing it to bring more and more pain into our lives and the lives of anyone around us. Choosing to suffer through withdrawals is actually the least painful choice we can and should make. It is all in how you look at it. This choice has to be made before you start doing without your source of addiction. Until you make up your mind, which is a huge part of the struggle itself, you will continue to suffer.

Try to view the struggles you go through as mini wars. With each struggle that you endure, you have just won a victory between the war of your mind and flesh. If you have determined in your spirit and made up your mind, the flesh is in complete opposition, so there is truly a war going on. No soldier wins victory without training and sometimes casualties. Keeping focused on your call and mission, preparing and disciplining yourselves will insure victory from our enemy's camp.

Let's examine some things that will help us realize there is a struggle, but there are also promises or advantages of being freed after we have suffered a little while. We are not in this battle alone, which is good because we cannot win it alone. If we could, wouldn't we be free by now? Don't dread the suffering, pain, or struggle. Instead, I want you to prepare for it, so that when it comes, you will be ready and not run at its onset. I want you to know and to be encouraged that the pain will end. You do not have to lose this battle again, but you do have to prepare.

We are guaranteed victory if we don't give up. You must stay focused on the prize of freedom, centered in Christ and grounded in His love. You must keep renewing your mind with the Word of God. Then, my friend, you will walk in the freedom you so long to have. If you do these things, even though you may not be ready for freedom from your addiction, you will come to the point of craving freedom and blessings more than you crave bondage. Trust me. It took almost a year to get my mind changed (transformed) into wanting freedom more than I wanted the addiction. I have fallen, failed, stumbled, or whatever else you want to call it many times since, but I am walking through freedom even today just as you will. We are in this together, you are not alone and there is hope.

One day as I was trying to distract myself from the pain of withdrawal from cigarettes, I was reading an article about losing weight. I want to share it because it wonderfully depicts the truth about how our bodies fight to hold on to whatever we have trained it to be addicted to. This excerpt is from Steve Edwards' article, "5 Ways to Keep the Scale Moving."

> Your body is a creature of habit, but it doesn't care whether those habits are bad or good. The more you do something to enact change, the more it adapts and tries to limit that change. This can be a good thing because less stress is placed on the body. But it's a bad thing if you're unhealthy because that is the state your body is willing to call homeostasis. If your goals are to change your body, you'll want to keep that adaptive stress high until you're fit and healthy.[1]

This article confirms what I felt and want to share. Your body will fight you when you deny it. By not giving in, you have a chance to become fit and healthy, which is the body's normal state. I am not warning you of this struggle to scare you but to prepare you. It is normal to fear change, but fear doesn't have to keep us from changing. When you know there is a bumpy road ahead on your way to Disneyland, you don't just give up your vacation; you tighten your seatbelt, lock the doors, and press through because you know it will be worth the trip. Freedom from addiction is even better than a vacation because you can enjoy it for the rest of your life. And you can extend that example of freedom to future generations.

Think of it this way. Let's say you give your dog a piece of steak every day for many years and then find out that if you continue to feed him that steak, you will kill him. You love your dog and want him to live and be happy, so you do what's best for him and go to take the steak from him. Your dog doesn't realize that what you are doing is for his own good; he feels you are denying him and being mean to him. Do you think that dog is going to release the steak to you without a fight? No, he will hold on with all his might because he has come to love it and has been trained to have it every day. There will be a struggle, not only when it is initially taken away but every day he sees you for a while. He will beg you for that steak and will be sad when he doesn't get it. Then one day you will notice that he doesn't beg as much or as long. Then you notice that your dog has more energy, his coat and teeth look healthier, and even his breath smells fresher. Even though there was an initial fight or struggle, it did decrease. In the end everyone was better off.

When we are in the midst of struggling with whether or not to give in to our addiction or go forward without it, there will be times when we give up and give in. When that happens and we have succumbed to our felt need; we come up feeling even emptier than before because whether it is drinking, smoking, drugs, cigarettes, sex, food, or gambling, it doesn't satisfy. It actually does the opposite, which is to make us only want more of it, thinking that if we had more, it would fill the void and need we have. If and when the struggle wins over the pursuit of freedom, see it for what it is: just a slip and not a complete downfall. The truth is that the need is still there, which is not going to be met by giving into our addiction but by abstaining from the harmful substance or behavior. We have two choices—go backwards or go forward.

If you are like me and fall into the temptation yet again, don't lose heart. You are not alone and it is not the end of the world. As quickly as you gave in to your temptation or addiction, you can turn and remember the truth and be set free. Freedom from addictions and any newly learned habit is a process. This process usually takes longer than we would like. It is during the wait that the desire to give up shows up. Each day we have another chance to make new choices. We can forget about our past mistakes, even the ones from five minutes ago, and decide that for this minute we will make better choices. If you take two steps forward and fall back one, you are still one step ahead of where you were. This equals progress. If you take one step forward, fall back two, you are still ahead because you would have fallen back the two anyway. Always look at the positive accomplishments instead of the negative pitfalls.

This Scripture encourages us that God understands our struggles and promises freedom and hope ahead.

> But in their time of trouble they cried to you, and you heard them from heaven. In your great mercy, you sent them liberators who rescued them from their enemies. But as soon as they were at peace, your people again committed

evil in your sight, and once more you let their enemies conquer them. Yet whenever your people turned and cried to you again for help, you listened once more from heaven. In your wonderful mercy, you rescued them many times!

—NEHEMIAH 9:27–28

I have had to be rescued many times. The key is to not give into your struggle, and if and when you do, don't let that temporary slip keep you down. Our enemies, which can be addictions, negative self-talk, setbacks, and even pride over how well we are doing, cause us to suffer even more than the temporary hardship our minds or bodies feel when they are not fed.

If you think you are standing strong, be careful not to fall. The temptations in your life are no different from what others experience. And God is faithful. He will not allow the temptation to be more than you can stand. When you are tempted, he will show you a way out so that you can endure.

—1 CORINTHIANS 10:12–13

This is usually what happens once we start walking in some freedom or after a few days of being able to stay clean, we start getting a little cocky about how we can do this on our own. Our attention and focus start to slip back to smoking, drugs, sex, cake, or mental strongholds. God will give us a way out, but sometimes we don't want to see it. We want to lie to ourselves that just one won't matter or we can quit again anytime we want to. I have fallen for that lie and have gotten trapped every time. Knowing it is a trap, don't even go close. Ask God to show you His way out and to strengthen you with endurance.

> "LORD, help!" they cried in their trouble, and he saved them from their distress. He sent out his word and healed them, snatching them from the door of death.
>
> —PSALM 107:19–20

I am calling out today. Won't you join me in crying out to God for freedom from our troubles and distresses, believing that God will hear and answer regardless of how many times you have had to cry out again for help?

> Now when the devil had ended every temptation, he departed from Him until an opportune time.
>
> —LUKE 4:13, NKJV

Just when you think you are doing well, Satan will be back with the lie that your addiction will fix your bad day or that it will bring a tangible feeling of comfort to your emotional pain. The relief you feel when you give into those lies is the relief from struggling, struggling whether or not to indulge. Once you have given in to your desire, the same old feelings of guilt and failure rise up even stronger. Be encouraged that we can even thank God when we fall because we are that much closer to seeing that these things don't truly satisfy but only hinder our lives. We can be strengthened to overcome the next temptation instead of beating ourselves up for slipping.

> And you will know the truth, and the truth will make you free.
>
> —JOHN 8:32

The more we come to know the Truth, the more we become free.

> So be truly glad. There is wonderful joy ahead, even though you have to endure many trials for a little while. These trials will show that your faith is genuine. It is being tested as fire tests and purifies gold—though your faith is far more precious than mere gold. So when your faith remains strong through many trials, it will bring you much praise and glory and honor on the day when Jesus Christ is revealed to the whole world.
>
> —1 PETER 1:6–7

I know that gladness is the last emotion you may feel when being tempted or going through withdrawals. However, we can turn our thinking around and be glad because with each withdrawal symptom or thought of giving in that we overcome; we are that much closer to freedom from bondage and having our lives controlled by something other than our addiction. In the end, we can look forward to much praise, glory, and honor. We must keep the prize, the reward, the good thing in front of us to help us endure.

> Of course, you get no credit for being patient if you are beaten for doing wrong. But if you suffer for doing good and endure it patiently, God is pleased with you.
>
> —1 PETER 2:20

> Remember, it is better to suffer for doing good, if that is what God wants, than to suffer for doing wrong!
>
> —1 PETER 3:17

> So then, since Christ suffered physical pain, you must arm yourselves with the same attitude he had, and be ready to suffer, too. For if you have suffered physically for Christ, you have finished with sin.
>
> —1 PETER 4:1

> Since he himself has gone through suffering and testing, he is able to help us when we are being tested.
>
> —HEBREWS 2:18

> Even though Jesus was God's Son, he learned obedience from the things he suffered.
>
> —HEBREWS 5:8

We can see in the above scriptures that suffering can occur for doing good or evil, the choice is ours. It seems like it would be an easy choice since we know that doing good is better than evil, but our flesh is strong. As I said earlier, sometimes in the midst of doing without cigarettes, I felt as though I would explode, literally. Other times, I felt like I will go crazy because my emotions were so out of control. You have probably been here as well if you have tried to walk away from your bondage. These feelings may get worse at times, but the good news is that they do disappear. They will lesson, until one day they are gone and you can apply this same mindset to any area of your life. Let's keep going to Jesus for His help, asking Him for the same mindset He had, and holding on to the promise that once we suffer for a little while, we will be done with that sin in our life! Amen!

> Therefore we also, since we are surrounded by so great a cloud of witnesses, let us lay aside every weight, and the sin which so easily ensnares us, and let us run with endurance the race that is set before us, looking unto Jesus, the author and finisher of our faith, who for the joy that was set before Him endured the cross, despising the shame, and has sat down at the right hand of the throne of God.
>
> —HEBREWS 12:1–2, NKJV

Join me in laying aside the mental weight of fear of failure, fear of suffering, fear of not having fun, and the fear of having messed up too many times and for too long. Get rid of the wrong thinking that you won't have to suffer to be free and the lie that you will suffer less by staying in your addiction. Let's run this race together, looking unto Jesus, enduring whatever comes our way, knowing that there is joy at the end of this journey. There is a payday. There are benefits to our struggle if we just don't give up. Notice I didn't say if we don't slip, fall, or make mistakes. I am Queen of Mistakes, but thank God He can use these mistakes to teach me and to help others.

Just this morning, I had to wrestle between wanting freedom or wanting to go back into my old lifestyle of smoking and getting high. (Yes, you will still be tempted regardless of how long you have been free. However, with each temptation comes the opportunity to flee.) I felt like bowing down to my urges to go to the store to buy cigarettes or (I can't believe I am admitting to this nasty thing) going to the ashtray to find a decent size butt to smoke. As I was wrestling with these thoughts and urges, I saw this scripture:

> It is for freedom that Christ has set us free. Stand firm, then, and do not let yourselves be burdened again by a yoke of slavery.
>
> —GALATIANS 5:1, NIV

> For when we died with Christ we were set free from the power of sin.
>
> —ROMANS 6:7

Regardless of how strong the struggle, it is clear that we don't have to give in to it or be controlled by it. We are no longer slaves, we are set free from its power and don't have to give into our sinful desires. No matter how loud and long they scream that we do have to give in or we will die, we can remind ourselves that the above scriptures tell us we are free. I know that may sound a little dramatic, but that is really how I feel at times about my nicotine withdrawals, which experts say are the worst type of addiction to break. But your addiction is probably just as hard for you to break as nicotine is for me.

So, now that we see there is a struggle, that it's common to all men and that we don't have to bow down to it, let's pray and ask for help. We will need help when the urges attack us like a fierce bulldog attacks, remembering that we are free and that this struggle will end—*if* we don't succumb to its demands.

As I was writing this book, walking through my withdrawals from many sins and attempting to walk through grief over my husband's death, I received this word of encouragement from Mike Murdock, which I want to share with you:

> Your struggles matter greatly to me. Every champion has discovered that pain is seasonal. Pain will pass. Pain is the passage to promotion. Midnight is almost over. A new day is about to dawn in your life. "Weeping may endure for a night, but joy cometh in the morning," (Psalm 30:5b). I am honored to be your prayer partner…and am expecting Miracles with you!

Let's pray.

Dear Lord,

I thank You for Your truth, which does in fact set us free. Help me to renew my mind with Your unfailing word so that the loud and ever present lies will lose their hold on my thinking and choices. I know I can't do anything apart from You, and I ask Your forgiveness for even trying. Strengthen me for difficulties, Lord, and enable me to endure the battle ahead, persevere when I want to give up, and cry for help daily without guilt. Thank You, Lord, that You understand my struggles. Thank You that You have done the hard part, which was to overcome sin once and for all. Thank You that I am not alone in this struggle.

In Jesus' name I pray. Amen.

Chapter 3

You Can't Have Just One

D O YOU REMEMBER THE COMMERCIAL FOR LAYS Potato Chips when they said, "betcha can't eat just one"? Every time I eat those things, I think of that saying and how true it is. I have even tried to eat just one, but to no avail. How many times have we said, "OK, just one more pack of cigarettes, just one more toke, just one more binge, just one more drink, just one more whatever"? I know I have said that more times than I can count. Just this last pack of cigarettes and then I can taper off, get lozenges, and finally be free.

I've been there, done that, and have the T-shirt to prove it. We both know that it's never just one more. That's what we tell ourselves to appease our flesh and to continue with what we think is the easy way out, which isn't easy at all. The whole time we are doing that "just one more," we are thinking about the dread we feel about having to give the addiction up. The fear of failure starts to set in about how this time will be no different than the last. We will try real hard or hardly try, and fail again.

The truth of the matter is that we really don't want just one. We want a whole lifetime of satisfying that need we feel when our old companion isn't with us anymore—our companion of death. You know the feeling, that feeling of grief, emptiness, and uneasiness when our body doesn't get what we have conditioned it to have every day and sometimes all day long. We want to continue in our habit of avoiding pain, avoiding reality, and especially avoiding another failure. We think it's easier to give into the temptation than it is to give ourselves over to a loving God who assures us freedom. We feel it's easier to give into our old way of thinking and dealing with our problems than to take on a new way of thinking, doing, and being.

As dysfunctional as it is, we believe that we can stay in our addiction because we are comfortable there. We know that is absurd, but we must face the truth of our thoughts. It is more comfortable in the moment to stay in our addiction because it pacifies our screaming flesh. Just like crying babies being weaned from the bottle or pacifier. They are not happy when it is taken away. They have had it their whole life, want it, think they need it, and will scream until they get it. As parents, we know that giving into their screaming will only hurt their development and maturity. Giving into their crying will only hinder and prolong their suffering. Every time we give in to the "just one more" lie, we are prolonging our suffering. It will keep us from experiencing the freedom of enjoying better ways to gratify our needs. Just like giving babies a pacifier or bottle past the appropriate age can cause damage to their mouth and teeth, giving into our addiction causes damage to us physically and mentally.

As parents, we want what's best for our children. God, the Father, is no different. Just because we scream and cry and it's hard, He is not being mean to us by saying these things need to go. He is telling us there is a better way, a better plan, a better future free of "must haves" in order to cope and live.

If you are still in the "just one more" phase, this is where we need to begin to seek God and ask Him for His strength to desire freedom. Every time I smoke, I am talking to God about delivering me and giving me a desire to be free yet again. I am asking Him to show me His way of escape and His timing. We can plan, desire, and make our minds up again to quit after this one last time, but it doesn't seem to work. The reason is because we are trying to do things in our way, in our own strength, and in our timing. Remember that apart from Jesus, we can do nothing, but what is impossible with man is possible with God. (See Matthew 19:26, NKJV.)

What does the Bible have to say about "just one more"?

> Instead, clothe yourself with the presence of the Lord Jesus Christ. And don't let yourself think about ways to indulge your evil desires.
>
> —ROMANS 13:14, NLT

> But put on the Lord Jesus Christ, and make no provision for the flesh, to fulfill its lusts.
>
> —ROMANS 13:14, NKJV

Both are excellent instructions on dealing with addictions. We have to stop thinking about our addiction, which includes ways to get free or ways to keep it going. As with anything else we have talked about in this book, it must first start with Jesus. Begin by practicing talking to Him as if He is right beside you. *Jesus, help me to acknowledge that You are with me wherever I go.*

We must always remember that we are involving Jesus in everything we do, even the sins of addiction we are participating in—smoking, drugs, sex, overspending, or whatever. As sickening as that may seem, because we are one with Jesus, that is what we are doing. He will never leave us or forsake us, so where do we think He goes when we are indulging ourselves with wrong and harmful things? Remember, we are not staying here. We are on a journey to freedom with our Lord. I am not saying these things to add more guilt to our guilt-ridden lives. I want to give us a bigger arsenal to fight these negative thought patterns that keep us in our present condition. Our thinking got us into this mess, and it will need to change to get us out.

The second part of verse 14 of Romans 13 (NLT) tells us, "And don't let yourself think about ways to indulge your evil desires." For me that's a tall order. I don't know about you, but I think about indulging my flesh a lot. I think about it and then I too often act on it. Sometimes I don't even think on it but just act on it from pure habit. Then I think about why I just did what I didn't want to do.

> For what I am doing, I do not understand. For what I will to do, that I do not practice; but what I hate, that I do.
>
> —ROMANS 7:14, NKJV

Even Paul struggled with the same problems and thoughts. That encourages me. This is the part where we have to think about what we are thinking and change it. Did you get that? We must not let ourselves think about ways to indulge our flesh. Again, this stuff sounds so easy but we both know that it is not easy. It takes time and practice, just like our addiction does and did. So what do we do when we fall into that same old trap of thinking about our addiction? We change what we think about.

> And now, dear brothers and sisters, one final thing. Fix your thoughts on what is true, and honorable, and right, and pure, and lovely, and admirable. Think about things that are excellent and worthy of praise.
>
> —PHILIPPIANS 4:8

We can't always control what pops into our minds but we can control what stays there. Just because I think about my addiction doesn't mean I have to dwell on it, meditate on it, and let it take up residence there. I can make a decision to say, "Well, that's not good, noble, or admirable, so help me, Lord, to think on something different such as freedom and the better health, self-respect, confidence, and extra time and money I am going to have."

> Stay alert! Watch out for your great enemy, the devil. He prowls around like a roaring lion, looking for someone to devour. Stand firm against him, and be strong in your faith. Remember that your Christian brothers and

sisters all over the world are going through the same kind of suffering you are. In his kindness God called you to share in his eternal glory by means of Christ Jesus. So after you have suffered a little while, he will restore, support, and strengthen you, and he will place you on a firm foundation.

—1 PETER 5:8–10

The first line of that scripture says to stay alert. It's so easy to just think on whatever comes to mind and run with it. When we are alert to our thoughts, we can bring them into line with God's Word and God's way of thinking. Again, this takes time and practice. Wars are not won overnight, and, my friends, we are in a war with ourselves. The good news is that we are assured victory in this war and we are given everything we need to win it. But, daily we must make the choice to pick up and use the weapons we are given. It does no good to ignore our enemy in hopes that our gun will automatically shoot and scare him off. We have to pick up, aim, and fire our mental weapons—sometimes many times an hour. The more we do it, the more the enemy will scatter and the more battlegrounds we will pick up.

I've heard it said that you have to start by quitting. For me that was a powerful statement. I thought that if it was that easy, I would have quit by now; but it's right. The first step is to make our mind up, pray for help, and then quit. We have to start somewhere. That first step is the hardest, but isn't that the case with anything in life that's worth having? So when the thought comes that we will quit next week after the holidays, we are entertaining the "just one" lie. Next week, tomorrow, or January 1 are all ways of procrastinating our freedom. Does that make sense? It will only be harder, not easier, the longer we put up with our addiction. Addictions are *not* our friends.

Remember the scripture in Romans 13:14 (NKJV) where it tells us to "make no provision for the flesh"? In terms of addictions, let's get real and practical with this instruction. Making no provision for the flesh means not to provide what you need in order to indulge your particular addiction. For me, that would mean to not buy cigarettes, to wash and put away the ashtrays, to get rid of the lighters, and to stop going to my familiar smoking areas. Even though drinking is not my issue, this also includes not even thinking about going to a bar to drink because I know doing that would cause me to want to smoke. For drug users, that means getting rid of your pipes, matches, baggies, dealers' phone numbers, and even your drug buddies you get high with. This may sound extreme but that's what it will take to get serious about having a good life full of freedom. We go to many extremes to meet our addiction so let's not think we can do any less for our journey to freedom.

If your addiction is to food, stop buying the Little Debbies, Hershey bars, cake mixes (regardless of what a great sale it is), or bags of cookies or chips. How can you binge on what's not there? Don't try to justify your purchases by telling yourself you will spend more at a convenience store. You will eventually get to the point of seeing your choice of freedom from addiction as more appealing than your choice to stay in bondage.

If your addiction is sexual vice, destroy the magazines, catalogs, and tapes. If you have a closet or drawer full of porn, get rid of it. I suggest you completely destroy all tapes and magazines so that they don't fall in the wrong hands and cause someone else to suffer from this widespread addiction. For the alcoholics, the beer or liquor needs to be poured out. Even that bottle of champagne you have been saving for that special occasion can be given away.

Please don't underestimate the draw these things have on you. Get rid of them. You can hear them call your name if you are even close to the same room, so they have to go. Now is not the time to think you are strong enough to withstand their ever-present lure. The time will come when addiction has no power over you, but it's not now.

Am I being a bossy know-it-all? No! I am sharing with you what it has taken for me to walk away from drugs, alcohol, sexual immorality, and gluttony. I too have to practice these same things when I find myself slipping back into old mind-sets and patterns. None of us are perfect, which is why we all need a Savior and His daily forgiveness. I am doing these same things so I understand the way an addict thinks and how hard it is to break the pattern. You are not alone. There is hope in finding freedom. It is possible.

Will it happen today, tomorrow, next year? God knows that answer but we shouldn't focus on the when, only the how. Of course, the sooner we face our addiction, the better. You will be free but the timing is not the determining factor. That is between you and God but He is rooting for you every day and every step of the way. Every day you don't quit going to God about your struggle is a day of victory. Every day you repent of your wrong actions and ask Him for help is a day closer to freedom from your vice. Every day you lackadaisically give into thoughts of feeding your addiction without so much as a glance towards freedom is another day stolen from you and your loved ones. Don't let that happen any longer. Satan has stolen from us long enough!

Addictions bring death to my soul, my confidence, my lungs, and my heart. I am praying each time I surrender to my fleshly lust: *God, this is not good for me. Please help me to live the life You died for me to have, which is a life free from any outside thing controlling me.* I am going to God for deliverance, for help, for strength and for the desire to put down my chosen vice once again. It is a daily choice. God has been with me every step of the way, and I know He will not give up on me no matter how much I deserve it. He is love.

Would you give up on your child that you love? Certainly not! Because of God's faithfulness, not our unfaithfulness, He will see us through this complicated matter of addiction. There is no doubt in my mind that we will be delivered and brought through this "Red Sea" of poor choice we call addiction. No matter how big the enemy, our God is bigger. Even now, I am seeking God for His master plan of freedom.

I don't know about you, but I am a planner and a doer. I can come up with some great ideas and make things happen. That is a good thing, but it can also be to my detriment if I leave God out of it and try to do things in my own strength. This usually ends in disappointment and yet another failure to add to my list. We need to confess that in and of ourselves, we are hopeless apart from God. Let's ask God for a love for our own selves to match the love He has for us. In doing that, we will not want to poison our minds and bodies with harmful choices. That may sound selfish that we need to love our selves, but the reality is that we are lacking in self-love. Loving parents would never their give their babies something that they know would bring destruction to their lives.

> He said, "That you love the Lord your God with all your passion and prayer and muscle and intelligence—and that you love your neighbor as well as you do yourself."
>
> —LUKE 10:27, THE MESSAGE

Maybe you are in the place of not even knowing this God I speak of, therefore it is impossible for you to love Him. Maybe you know Him from a distance, but not really. You may know Him but still don't love yourself. God knows all things and accepts us wherever we are on our journey. He requires us to worship Him in "spirit and in truth" (John 4:24). Since we all have to start somewhere, we start with honesty. Go to Him in prayer regardless of where you are. An example would be: *God, I don't know You and am not even convinced I want to, help me. God, You seem so far away, please become personal to me. Lord, I don't like myself, much less love myself. Change my heart and thinking.* When we go to Him and ask, He will hear and answer.

Keep in mind that the earth may not tremble and shake and your whole world change overnight, even though with

God all things are possible. Faith means believing without seeing. He promises that when we draw near to Him, He *will* draw near to us. If we seek Him, we *will* find Him, if we seek Him with our whole heart. Our attitude and the object of our affection must be changed from our addiction to an addiction to Jesus.

Please join me in my heartfelt prayer to put on Jesus and make no provision for the flesh. Prayer is a personal, one-on-one conversation with God. Use this prayer as a starting point, realizing there is no "magic" prayer. This is my prayer. I invite you to join me, but I still encourage you to personalize it with your personality and specific situation.

> *Dear Lord Jesus,*
>
> *I have and continue to make provision for my flesh by buying and having harmful things in my possession. I know I need to start somewhere at some point, so today please lead me and show me Your plan, path, and timing. I will commit my way of continuing to hurt myself to You. You promise that when I commit my way to You, You will direct my paths. Direct me into freedom. Forgive me for continuing this cycle of giving in to harmful and destructive patterns. Forgive me for not loving myself enough to do the very best for me. Change me, Lord. Give me strength and hope. Fill me with a desire to love You and me. I am tired of hurting myself and others with my choices. I am tired of choosing death over life. I pray for wisdom to make a fresh start with different choices. You*

have a good plan for my life. Help me to walk in that good plan. You tell me if I ask You for godly wisdom, You will give it to me; so I ask now for godly wisdom, wisdom to know what is the right thing to do and the right way to do it. Thank You that You are not ashamed of me or hate me because I keep messing up. I want to know and experience all the love You have for me. Help me, God. I need You! This is the day You have made, so I will be glad and rejoice in it. Let me be glad You are for me and not against me. Let me rejoice in Your promise of freedom. I surrender my plans to You. I surrender my thinking and choices to You. I surrender doing things in my own strength to You. Show me who You are and Your ways that I may walk in them and prosper. God, I thank You and praise You for what I don't see yet, which is freedom from addiction. You are not man that You should lie. Thank You, Lord. By faith I say I love You and therefore I love myself.

In Jesus' name I pray. Amen.

Chapter 4

LET'S TALK ABOUT SEX

S O WHAT'S WRONG WITH SEX? IT FEELS GOOD, IT'S fun, and it's natural. How can something that feels so good be so bad? First of all, sex in and of itself is not bad. God came up with the idea of sex and created the parts we need to have amazing intimacy with our partners. Like all things in life, God has given us boundaries, which He put in place for our own good and safety. These boundaries are not meant to withhold pleasure from us. In order to be fulfilled and have true pleasure in any area of our lives, we need to obey God.

Why should we want to stay within those boundaries? The idea of waiting until marriage to have sex or make love is almost unheard of these days, but it is still God's plan. Having sex outside of marriage brings hurt, brings possible disease and unwanted pregnancy, as well as emotional baggage into a relationship.

Most times after engaging in sexual addictions, shame and disgust set in. Self-indulgence of any type may leave a temporary satisfaction, but then the urge returns, many times even stronger. Maybe you're not even bothered by what you keep doing, but you realize it is never enough. You feel empty and incomplete and just not sure why. It may satisfy for a moment but then you want it again and again.

That's how all sin is. It gives us a temporary feeling of pleasure but then leaves us feeling empty and used up and wanting more to get that feeling of satisfaction. Have you ever noticed that the satisfaction just keeps getting harder and harder to fulfill? The more we feed this type of behavior, the more we need, which is why it's an addiction. The more we do without it and turn our thoughts elsewhere, the easier it is to do without it. We begin to feel more energized by being clean and not giving in to our flesh and sexual desires.

Sin will never fully satisfy our deep desire for being wanted and loved, which is truly what we are seeking with sex. We want to feel wanted, satisfied, and content, but that feeling evades us when met according to our own ways versus God's ways. He is the only one who can truly meet those deep internal needs we have. Even men, whose needs are more physical than emotional, are trying to be in control instead of relinquishing control to the Creator.

> My dear children, let's not just talk about love; let's practice real love. This is the only way we'll know we're living truly, living in God's reality. It's also the way to shut down debilitating self-criticism, even when there is something to it. For God is greater than our worried hearts and knows more about us than we do ourselves.
>
> And friends, once that's taken care of and we're no longer accusing or condemning

ourselves, we're bold and free before God! We're able to stretch our hands out and receive what we asked for because we're doing what he said, doing what pleases him. Again, this is God's command: to believe in his personally named Son, Jesus Christ. He told us to love each other, in line with the original command. As we keep his commands, we live deeply and surely in him, and he lives in us. And this is how we experience his deep and abiding presence in us: by the Spirit he gave us.

—1 JOHN 3:19–21, THE MESSAGE

So, how do we overcome these controlling thoughts of sex, the desire to view porn, or look at people with lustful thoughts? Even though this seems like a physical problem, it is basically a mental one which affects the body. You don't commit adultery without first lusting after the person and then fantasizing about being with them. You don't just view porn without thinking about it first. Since it starts with your thoughts, it must also end with your thoughts. At the onset of these images, ideas, and plans, we must speak out loud to Jesus asking Him to purify our thoughts and change our desires to His desires, His purity, and His way of doing things. The feelings will still be there until you do this for quite a while and get into the habit of *not* giving in to these lustful practices. The more you abstain, the less you *have* to fulfill that desire, which is a reward in itself. This process may be a lengthy one, but it will be worth the freedom. What we are looking for can only be fulfilled according to God's way of doing things, not ours. When we truly believe that doing things our way instead of God's way brings us harm, then we will begin to desire His ways instead.

> There are six things the LORD hates—no, seven things he detests: haughty eyes, a lying tongue, hands that kill the innocent, a heart that plots evil, feet that race to do wrong, a false witness who pours out lies, a person who sows discord in a family.
>
> —PROVERBS 6:16–19

Many people, usually those who don't struggle with the sin of sexual addiction, judge those who do. Based on the above scripture, judgment is listed as one of the things the Lord hates. A sin that we don't personally struggle with is always worse than our own, or so we are deceived into thinking. For your own sakes, please don't judge a brother or sister who suffers from any type of sexual sin. Your part is to love, pray for, forgive, and encourage them. God is the judge, not us. Our society tends to judge homosexuality as a huge sin. According to scripture, it is a sin, but so is judgment. God has shown me that the same blood that cleanses me of all my sin, cleanses His children of homosexuality. There is hope, healing, and forgiveness for any type of sin. I have heard people say that they are born a homosexual. Are we also born murderers, adulterers, liars, cheaters, or stealers? Sin is sin and needs to be forgiven.

Let's look at some of the scriptures regarding specific sexual sins. We will start with homosexuality. I am no expert, only someone wanting to bring hope and healing to a hurting world through the love and truth of God's perfect Word.

> And the men, instead of having normal sexual relations with women, burned with lust for each other. Men did shameful things with other men, and as a result of this sin, they suffered within themselves the penalty they deserved. Since they thought it foolish to acknowledge God, he abandoned them to their foolish thinking and let them do things that should never be done. Their lives became full of every kind of wickedness, sin, greed, hate, envy, murder, quarreling, deception, malicious behavior, and gossip.
>
> —ROMANS 1:27–29

> …as Sodom and Gomorrah, and the cities around them in a similar manner to these, having given themselves over to sexual immorality and gone after strange flesh, are set forth as an example, suffering the vengeance of eternal fire. Likewise also these dreamers defile the flesh, reject authority, and speak evil of dignitaries.
>
> —JUDE 1:7–9, NKJV

The wages of sin are death, and we want life and freedom. God loves us and doesn't want us to be controlled by our sinful desires. He has made a way for us to be free through the once and for all sacrifice of Jesus. When we believe in Him and confess our sins to Him, we will be set free. Please look at these scriptures as an invitation for freedom, not to turn your back on His truth because you can't or don't want to change.

> Whoever commits adultery with a woman lacks understanding; He who does so destroys his own soul. Wounds and dishonor he will get, and his reproach will not be wiped away.
>
> —PROVERBS 6:32–33, NKJV

> You have heard that it was said to those of old, "You shall not commit adultery." But I say to you that whoever looks at a woman to lust for her has already committed adultery with her in his heart.
>
> —MATTHEW 5:27–28, NKJV

> But I say to you that whoever divorces his wife for any reason except sexual immorality causes her to commit adultery; and whoever marries a woman who is divorced commits adultery.
>
> —MATTHEW 5:32, NKJV

The hope for anyone who has committed adultery or sexual sin of any kind is that Jesus died for us to be forgiven of any and all sin. I invite you to confess your sin and receive forgiveness and cleansing, not condemnation, which is sin as well. If you are even toying with thoughts, looking lustfully at a coworker or someone in your church, looking at porn or magazines, or whatever and you are married, that is adultery. Please go to the Lord now before it goes any further. Distance yourself from the temptation. Put no confidence in the flesh. That means don't trust yourself, no matter how holy or moral you think you are. Lust and sexual sins are very strong. Look at the news; preachers, pastors, priests, and ministers are not above temptation and usually are attacked very strongly in this area. So don't play with fire, you will get burned.

> I can hardly believe the report about the sexual immorality going on among you—something that even pagans don't do. I am told that a man in your church is living in sin with his stepmother.
>
> —1 CORINTHIANS 5:1

> Now the body is not for sexual immorality but for the Lord, and the Lord for the body.
>
> —1 CORINTHIANS 6:13, NKJV

> Nevertheless I have a few things against you, because you allow that woman Jezebel, who calls herself a prophetess, to teach and seduce My servants to commit sexual immorality and eat things sacrificed to idols. And I gave her time to repent of her sexual immorality, and she did not repent. Indeed I will cast her into

a sickbed, and those who commit adultery with her into great tribulation, unless they repent of their deeds.

—REVELATION 2:20–22, NKJV

Neither fornicators, nor idolaters, nor adulterers, nor homosexuals, nor sodomites, nor thieves, nor covetous, nor drunkards, nor revilers, nor extortioners will inherit the kingdom of God. And such were some of you. But you were washed, but you were sanctified, but you were justified in the name of the Lord Jesus and by the Spirit of our God. All things are lawful for me, but all things are not helpful. All things are lawful for me, but I will not be brought under the power of any. Foods for the stomach and the stomach for foods, but God will destroy both it and them. Now the body is not for sexual immorality but for the Lord, and the Lord for the body. And God both raised up the Lord and will also raise us up by His power. Do you not know that your bodies are members of Christ? Shall I then take the members of Christ and make them members of a harlot? Certainly not! Or do you not know that he who is joined to a harlot is one body with her? For "the two," He says, "shall become one flesh." But he who is joined to the Lord is one spirit with Him. Flee sexual immorality. Every sin that a man does is outside the body, but he who commits sexual immorality sins against his own body. Or do you not know that your body is the temple of the Holy Spirit who is in you, whom you have from God, and you are not your own? For you were bought at a price; therefore glorify God in your body and in your spirit, which are God's.

—1 Corinthians 6:9–20, nkjv

Marriage is honorable among all, and the bed undefiled; but fornicators and adulterers God will judge.

—Hebrews 13:4, nkjv

Now we have established and defined what sexual immorality is. Some of us have been miserable without even knowing why, and it has been because we live a life of sexual immorality. The above scriptures were written to the church, which proves that just because you are a Christian, it doesn't exempt you from being tempted by or involved with sexual sins. God wants us free, even in this life, from the consequences of sin. We see it brings curses upon us, it hurts our bodies and the Lord, and is not good for us. None of us truly want to be in bondage. I will be the first to admit that sin feels good, for a moment, but afterwards we are left feeling empty, used, abused, shamed, and guilt laden. That is nothing close to freedom.

Where do we go from here? What do we do when we burn with desires? I'll be the first to admit that I have committed many sexual sins. But I know that Jesus wants His bride pure and spotless and undefiled. That is all of our desire because we have the perfect seed of Christ living in us; our born-again spirits desire that purity. But then we have our flesh that wages war against the things of God. God always gives us boundaries and gives us a way out of temptation. If and when we fall into (or actively pursue) sin, let us never forget that we have an advocate named Jesus who is willing and able to forgive us.

> My little children, these things I write to you, so that you may not sin. And if anyone sins, we have an Advocate with the Father, Jesus Christ the righteous. And He Himself is the propitiation for our sins, and not for ours only but also for the whole world.
>
> —1 JOHN 2:1–2, NKJV

When we sin, we must confess and repent, but we want to be to the point of not sinning at all. What does scripture say about sexual immorality and how to get away from it? We'll begin with a scripture for married people who may have the opposite problem, which is withholding sex from their spouse. God is in favor of sexual relations. He is the one who created us to enjoy that purpose with pleasure, but with all things there are boundaries He places for our own good.

> The wife does not have authority over her own body, but the husband does. And likewise the husband does not have authority over his own body, but the wife does. Do not deprive one another except with consent for a time, that you may give yourselves to fasting and prayer;

and come together again so that Satan does
not tempt you because of your lack of self-
control. But I say this as a concession, not as a
commandment.

—1 Corinthians 7:4–6, nkjv

The same grace and deliverance is available for this type
of sexual immorality as well. We are not to withhold sex from
our spouse because we are tired, didn't get that diamond
bracelet we wanted, or are mad because they are acting like
a jerk. Hopefully you have a spouse who understands these
things and will be forgiving, but that is not always the case.
Pray for them and leave the results in God's hands; but you
must do your part, which is to honor your spouse with your
body. It is also important not to hold the lack of sex over
a spouse's head as the reason they have cheated or watched
porn or anything else. We are all responsible for our own
choices, period. Also, we are to submit according to Jesus
who does not condone group sex, orgies, porn, or any other
type of perverted sexual activity a spouse may try to bring
into your marriage bed. If you don't have peace about it,
don't do it. This goes for the man or woman. Some women
are the perpetrators of sexual perversion.

God gives us specific instructions and boundaries for
all things, so we need to search to learn how to break free.
Any time we fall short or fail, we have to confess, repent, and
ask for God's help in following His instructions. Know that
God is faithful to forgive me and cleanse me of all unrighteousness. It is best to flee from the sin instead of needing to
repent, but we must start where we are.

Flee sexual immorality.

—1 CORINTHIANS 6:18, NKJV

For this is the will of God, your sanctification: that you should abstain from sexual immorality; that each of you should know how to possess his own vessel in sanctification and honor.

—1 THESSALONIANS 4:3–4, NKJV

Flee also youthful lusts; but pursue righteousness, faith, love, peace with those who call on the Lord out of a pure heart.

—2 TIMOTHY 2:22, NKJV

The weapons we fight with are not the weapons of the world. On the contrary, they have divine power to demolish strongholds. We demolish arguments and every pretension that sets itself up against the knowledge of God, and we take captive every thought to make it obedient to Christ.

—2 CORINTHIANS 10:4–5, NIV

We must flee, run from, and not stay in the same room with our temptation. I know these things are easier said than done, and I personally have failed miserably, but we must acknowledge that today is a new day. Join with me in forgetting what lies behind and pressing towards Jesus. (See Philippians 3:13–14.)

We are to pursue and go after righteousness instead of a

new video, magazine, or boyfriend or girlfriend to sleep with. Right at the onset of thoughts about sex in an immoral way, we are to bring those thoughts to Jesus. At the onset! If you indulge yourself in this type of thinking, it may be impossible to reel in your emotions. Get away from the temptation and talk to Jesus about what you are thinking and feeling. Getting into this habit will eventually bring relief. Remember that you may just need to start by asking for the desire for purity. Maybe God is dealing with you about something else right now. By spending time with Him, all things will be taken care of in His timing. Be patient.

> Keep watch and pray, so that you will not give in to temptation. For the spirit is willing, but the body is weak!
>
> —Matthew 26:41

If sexual vice is our weakness, we need to watch our thought life that it doesn't get out of hand and pray for help in this area. I have won and lost battles but because of Jesus' sacrifice and forgiveness, I know the war has been won.

> So, if you think you are standing firm, be careful that you don't fall! No temptation has seized you except what is common to man. And God is faithful; he will not let you be tempted beyond what you can bear. But when you are tempted, he will also provide a way out so that you can stand up under it.
>
> —1 Corinthians 10:12–13, niv

> Do kill (deaden, deprive of power) the evil
> desire lurking in your members [those animal
> impulses and all that is earthly in you that is
> employed in sin]: sexual vice, impurity, sensual
> appetites, unholy desires, and all greed and
> covetousness, for that is idolatry (the deifying of
> self and other created things instead of God).
>
> —COLOSSIANS 3:5, AMP

Aren't you tired of being controlled by your thoughts and impulses to have sexual satisfaction? It's never enough. You must deprive it of its power by *not* giving in. You *ignore* the impulse. Walk away. Talk to Jesus. Praise His name. Realize your sexual organs, thoughts, and impulses are not your master and they will decrease every time you ignore the impulse to give in.

When we are burning with desire, it may feel like there is no turning back, but that is a lie. The above scripture says God won't give us more than what we can bear. Giving in and making bad choices will not only hurt our self-worth and self-esteem, the immoral relationships will end up leaving us crushed and hurt us and our loved ones. I have to say again, that God does not want to withhold any good thing from us. He wants to give us life, protection, and purity, which bring joy and peace instead of shame and turmoil.

Let's pray together.

Lord Jesus,
I have sinned against You repeatedly with my
body and mind. Please forgive me. When I burn

with passion and lust, I see how that hurts me and my relationships. Help me to bring my thoughts captive to You when they invade my mind, enable me to desire to get rid of all tempting materials that feed my lust, and help me to flee from situations which tempt me. Help me to do what is pleasing in Your sight and best for me. Even when I want to do what's right, my old nature runs backwards. Please give me discernment, Lord, that I may run to You instead. Thank You for helping me, freeing me, cleansing me, and changing me.

In Jesus' name I pray. Amen.

Chapter 5

I Can't Believe I Ate the Whole Thing

SINCE THIS BOOK IS ABOUT ADDICTIONS, I CAN'T LEAVE out the addiction to food. Although food addiction isn't always followed by obesity, you can see how widespread (no pun intended) this epidemic is by observing how many overweight people there are anyplace you go. Gluttony is simply the habit or act of eating too much. That definition describes most of us at one point or another, but a true glutton is someone who does this habitually, not just at an all-you-can-eat buffet.

Another indicator of a glutton would be when we don't feel we have the freedom to not eat. For me, regardless of how full I felt, if the food was good, I felt obligated to eat until it was gone or I was about to vomit. Most people have the ability or freedom to eat a couple of cookies or a small piece of cake. But a glutton would feel compelled to eat it all, or at least until it was physically impossible to shove in any more. The only reason I don't weigh two hundred pounds is because I am active and have received God's grace and wisdom towards food.

For many years I had a pull towards food. I used to say that I could hear sweets calling my name from the kitchen. I would dream of food. I would lust after sweets, cookies, cakes, and pies. Night eating was always worse because, for some reason, I couldn't seem to get full. I could literally eat for hours. I prayed for many, many years about the pull food had on me. It was lust.

Like any addiction, we can use food to fill not only our stomachs but also our emotions. We use it to comfort us when we are stressed, fill our time when we are bored, or reward ourselves when we have done something good or accomplished a hard task. Food can be used as a tool to quiet our anger, destroy our bodies that we secretly loathe, or as an attempt to become obese in hopes of keeping people away from us. I have heard that some people who have been sexually molested overeat in an attempt to protect themselves from someone wanting them that way again. Whatever the reason for our misuse of food, we can identify the root of it and begin to replace food with the comfort of God's love.

A common thread I have found with any addiction is the guilt associated after we have succumbed to our addictive habit. How many times have you binged and then looked in the mirror only to be consumed with guilt and self-hatred? Many times this is a vicious cycle. Do we binge to cover up the guilt and shame we feel, or do we feel guilt and shame because of the gluttony, or is it both? Regardless of the reason, God is and has the answer.

Jesus exchanges all our baggage of guilt, shame, sin, and fear for His life of freedom from sin. He has healed, cleansed, and delivered us. We just need to receive and walk in that freedom. We try on our own to cover or recover from these negative emotions with something temporal and immediate, which leads us down a path of destruction instead of deliverance. Because of our impatience, we want comfort now, regardless of the consequences. I know I do. Just recently I cried out to God for an immediate release from pain I was going through and when I didn't get my way, I turned to smoking. Then I began to feel guilty about that so I began eating garbage food, telling myself, "I don't care!" The truth is that we do care and so does God.

> Jesus told him, "I am the way, the truth, and the life. No one can come to the Father except through me."
>
> —JOHN 14:6

I think so many times we see scriptures about sin, especially the sin we struggle with, and feel condemned instead of inspired. I want to challenge us all to look at scriptures in a different light.

> All Scripture is inspired by God and is useful to teach us what is true and to make us realize what is wrong in our lives. It corrects us when we are wrong and teaches us to do what is right. God uses it to prepare and equip his people to do every good work.
>
> —2 TIMOTHY 3:16–17

The scripture below is warning us against drinking with drunkards and eating with gluttons. If you are either of those or both, you could find this very offensive. But realize that He starts with a term of endearment, "My child." Any good parent wants what's best for their child, such as hanging around people that will lift them up, not bring them down into bondage. Please know that all scripture is given to lift up and encourage, even if through correction and directness. When we are drunkards or gluttons, our hearts are not right because they are set on drinking and eating in excess. For me, that is where the lust was. I always lusted after more than my share, always in excess of what was good for me. We know based on other scriptures that God's will and desire is for us to use self-control and to prosper. We can take these warnings as words of love to keep us from being in poverty and wearing rags. We also know that even if we are a drunkard or a glutton, daily there is room for repentance.

> My child, listen and be wise: Keep your heart on the right course. Do not carouse with drunkards or feast with gluttons, for they are on their way to poverty, and too much sleep clothes them in rags.
>
> —PROVERBS 23:19–21

Another reason I was a glutton was because of fear. I feared not having enough or missing out on the good stuff, so I would eat in excess, especially if it was good. Scripture is full of verses that show that God supplies all of our needs, including food. It is a gift from Him. He gives us the gift of food to nourish us, refresh us, and give us strength. I believe it is also partly to show His love. When we are gluttonous, we are in essence saying we don't trust Him enough to supply our daily needs. We want more than our fair share.

In Exodus 16 it tells the story of the Israelites complaining to Moses about not having any food. God heard their complaints and decided to feed His children quail and rain down manna from heaven. They were given specific instructions to gather only what they needed for themselves and their families. Some gathered more than they needed and it bred worms and stank. They were afraid and did not believe that God would supply their needs. They wanted more than their fair share. That is what we do when we overindulge.

Read and meditate on the following scriptures and allow the love and promises of God's provision to strengthen you and change your heart—away from food to Him.

> They all depend on you to give them food as they need it. When you supply it, they gather it. You open your hand to feed them, and they are richly satisfied.
>
> —PSALM 104:27–28

> He causes us to remember his wonderful works. How gracious and merciful is our LORD! He gives food to those who fear him; he always remembers his covenant.
>
> —PSALM 111:4–5

He saved us from our enemies. His faithful love endures forever. He gives food to every living thing. His faithful love endures forever. Give thanks to the God of heaven. His faithful love endures forever.

—PSALM 136:24–26

I love the verses below because they give us hope when we have fallen into gluttony. When we are obese or even just overweight, we don't feel good mentally or physically. Then not only the load of the excess weight but also the load of guilt and shame bend us down. We can turn to God for help when we fall. We can ask Him to lift us up from beneath our loads, hope in Him, and trust Him that our need (not lust) for food will be supplied and that He will satisfy us. Have you ever noticed that satisfaction is *not* what you feel after eating too much or eating when you're not hungry? It's usually the opposite, which is dissatisfaction from being over-filled but not fulfilled. We are looking for satisfaction for our souls in food instead of our Creator.

The LORD helps the fallen and lifts those bent beneath their loads. The eyes of all look to you in hope; you give them their food as they need it. When you open your hand, you satisfy the hunger and thirst of every living thing.

—PSALM 145:14–16

He gives justice to the oppressed and food to the hungry. The LORD frees the prisoners. The

LORD opens the eyes of the blind. The LORD
lifts up those who are weighed down. The LORD
loves the godly.

—PSALM 146:7–8

By reading and meditating on these scriptures, we can
begin to thank God for His gift of provision of not only food
but also His love, His help, and His promise of taking care
of us. Many times we eat when we are worried. The scripture
below shows that we are valuable to the Lord. We matter to
Him and every single part of our lives matters to Him. He
doesn't even want us to worry about what our bodies look
like. Now that's a big one for most women and some men.
Just look at some of the shows on TV nowadays. Many shows
are based on what we look like, what to eat or not eat, or
what to wear or not wear. God wants our focus to be on Him
and to trust that He will supply all of our needs. These needs
include being loved, taken care of, fed, and clothed. When
we worry about these things, it just causes us more pain,
which often causes us to run to food for comfort. He wants
us running to Him instead.

That is why I tell you not to worry about everyday
life—whether you have enough food and drink,
or enough clothes to wear. Isn't life more than
food, and your body more than clothing? Look
at the birds. They don't plant or harvest or store
food in barns, for your heavenly Father feeds
them. And aren't you far more valuable to him

than they are? Can all your worries add a single moment to your life?

—MATTHEW 6:25–27

He told them to take nothing for their journey except a walking stick—no food, no traveler's bag, no money. He allowed them to wear sandals but not to take a change of clothes.

—MARK 6:8–9

Now how many of you would be cringing about right now if you were told to take a journey with no food and knowing that there would be no McDonalds on the way? I know that there was a time in my life when I would have gone into sheer panic! They couldn't take anything that would be used for self-care—no food, no makeup, no hairbrush, no tooth-brush, no snacks, no cokes. *Nothing!* Talk about trusting in God to supply all your needs! It may seem like a horrible place to be; but, in all honesty, what better place could there be than in the loving, caring hands of our Heavenly Father? Whether we acknowledge it or not, we are all dependent on God to provide grain for the animals, the rain for the crops, and the sun to cause it all to grow.

"Don't you understand either?" he asked. "Can't you see that the food you put into your body cannot defile you? Food doesn't go into your heart, but only passes through the stomach and then goes into the sewer." (By saying this, he declared that every kind of food is acceptable in God's eyes.) And then he added, "It is what comes from inside that defiles you.

—MARK 7:18–20

This scripture refers to our hearts. (See also Proverbs 23:19.) So many times we use food to try to meet the heartfelt needs we have instead of going to Jesus and allowing Him to meet those needs. Although in this passage it talks about food not defiling us but what's in our hearts. How many times have we seen food as the culprit? Food in and of itself is a gift from God; it's not bad or evil. Food is to be received with thanksgiving, not shunned. What defiles us is the attitude we have towards food. We try to control the food by counting fat grams, protein content, carbs or no carbs, sugar or saccharin, and on and on. God has given us the fruit of the Spirit, which includes self-control, not food control. We can ask for God to help us develop this fruit in our lives so that we can only eat when we are hungry and stop when we are full. We can ask for wisdom to choose healthy food that will nourish and strengthen our bodies instead of causing them to feel run down and become disease-laden.

If any of you lacks wisdom, let him ask of God, who gives to all liberally and without reproach, and it will be given to him. But let him ask in faith, with no doubting, for he who doubts is like a wave of the sea driven and tossed by the wind.

—JAMES 1:5–6, NKJV

Give us each day the food we need, and forgive
us our sins, as we forgive those who sin against
us. And don't let us yield to temptation.

—LUKE 11:3–4

According to the above scripture, we can ask for the food
we *need*, be forgiven our sin of gluttony, and ask for strength
not to yield to the temptation of overeating. I know I am
making this sound simple, and I acknowledge it is harder
than it sounds; but we can, little by little, change our focus
from food to God. By going to Him each and every time we
are tempted, we can reach the point where we can enjoy food
as the gift it is, not the god that controls us.

"But don't be so concerned about perishable
things like food. Spend your energy seeking the
eternal life that the Son of Man can give you.
For God the Father has given me the seal of his
approval."…Jesus told them, "This is the only
work God wants from you: Believe in the one
he has sent."

—JOHN 6:27, 29

Based on the above scripture, we know we are not to be
concerned about food. We are to spend our energy on seeking
Jesus. God has approved us, which meets our need of love and
affirmation. We have been seeking these things from food, but
enough is never enough. This scripture tells us what not to
do, what to do, and most importantly that God approves of
us. Our concern shouldn't be about food—what to eat or not

eat, how much or how little. We shouldn't concern or think or worry ourselves about that at all. Try thinking about Jesus and Him approving of you and having eternal life while you are thinking about a piece of cheesecake or cheeseburger. See how your focus will be on one or the other?

> For it seemed good to the Holy Spirit and to us to lay no greater burden on you than these few requirements: You must abstain from eating food offered to idols...
>
> —ACTS 15:28–29

May I suggest that when we eat junk all day, eat when we are not hungry, and continue to eat well after we know we are full, we are offering that food to the idol of our stomachs? You can call your stomach an idol, the lust for the food an idol, the food itself the idol, or the unmet emotional needs an idol. We can confess our sin of idolatry right now, ask for forgiveness, and replace Jesus on the throne of our heart where He belongs. We need to see that gluttony hurts us in so many ways, but that there is freedom from this bondage.

> Those who worship the Lord on a special day do it to honor him. Those who eat any kind of food do so to honor the Lord, since they give thanks to God before eating. And those who refuse to eat certain foods also want to please the Lord and give thanks to God. For we don't live for ourselves or die for ourselves.
>
> —ROMANS 14:6–7

How do we start over and change our habits? We turn to God in thanksgiving for our food. Include all food: meals, snacks and nibbles, thoughts of food, cleaning off the kids' plates, and even the lust over TV commercials about food. In everything we do, we do it unto the Lord. When your thoughts turn to food, turn them to the Lord. When your stomach growls, ask the Lord what He wants to eat. Before you pop that last morsel in your mouth, thank God and ask Him if He's still hungry.

> You say, "I am allowed to do anything"—but not everything is good for you. And even though "I am allowed to do anything," I must not become a slave to anything. You say, "Food was made for the stomach, and the stomach for food." (This is true, though someday God will do away with both of them.) But you can't say that our bodies were made for sexual immorality. They were made for the Lord, and the Lord cares about our bodies.
>
> —1 CORINTHIANS 6:12–13

As we can see in the above scripture, we *are free* to do whatever we want but only if it is not controlling us. Ask yourself these questions before you eat, "Am I really hungry? Is this healthy for me? Am I already full? Do I really want and need two helpings? Should I eat before I go to bed, knowing it will be stored as fat?"

> Jesus Christ is the same yesterday, today, and forever. So do not be attracted by strange, new

ideas. Your strength comes from God's grace, not from rules about food, which don't help those who follow them.

—HEBREWS 13:8–10

If I can thank God for the food and enjoy it, why should I be condemned for eating it? So whether you eat or drink, or whatever you do, do it all for the glory of God.

—1 CORINTHIANS 10:30–31

I listed these scriptures to warn us that *diets don't work*! Regardless of what the latest fad is—Atkins, South Beach, Weight Watchers, Quick Slim, or whatever comes out next— healthy eating and exercise is a daily choice and the only natural way of losing weight and keeping it off. The above diets will cause you to lose weight; but if your heart and atti- tude towards food hasn't changed, what happens when you go off the plan? That's right, the old patterns return and so does the weight. This is about freedom, not weight loss, but the two will go hand in hand.

So you also should consider yourselves to be dead to the power of sin and alive to God through Christ Jesus. Do not let sin control the way you live; do not give in to sinful desires. Do not let any part of your body become an instru- ment of evil to serve sin. Instead, give yourselves completely to God, for you were dead, but now you have new life. So use your whole body as an instrument to do what is right for the glory of God.

—ROMANS 6:11–13

We do not have to allow food to control our thoughts and bodies any longer. With each thought of food, bite, binge, or purge, we can turn to God in prayer, with thanksgiving, and begin to feast on His Word and love. He will change not only our bodies but our hearts as well. Regardless of how long you have been addicted to food, you can begin anew right now.

Let's pray.

Father,

Forgive me for allowing food to be my god and idol. Forgive me for giving in to gluttony to fill the needs that only You can fill. Forgive me for being fearful that You might not provide for my needs. Let me eat and drink with thanksgiving unto You. Let my meals be received and eaten to bring You glory. Thank You that You are not disappointed in me and that You love me and desire for me to be free. Help me to know that I am approved of by You. This is the day that You have made and I will be glad and rejoice in it. Thank You for new beginnings and new attitudes towards food, eating, and exercise. Be with me each day and teach me Your ways, Oh Lord, my God and My redeemer.

In Jesus' name I pray. Amen.

Chapter 6

LET ME HELP YOU

THIS CHAPTER IS FOR ANYONE WHO IS IN A RELAtionship with an addict, regardless of the addiction. It is also to help the addict to get an inside view on how their actions affect their loved ones. I grew up in an alcoholic home filled with chaos with no security or stability. I remember wanting so badly for my mom to quit drinking. Her actions had a devastating effect on our household, emotionally and financially. I can still recall the unimportance I felt when she would choose her drinking and partying over our well being. I couldn't understand how she loved her liquor more than she loved us. When you are in that type of situation, you feel helpless, hopeless, and worthless. Addicts choose the addiction over anything or anyone else because that is what is controlling their life.

As a former alcoholic and drug addict, I can understand the drive of getting your fix above all else. An addict would go to the store no matter what for a cigarette but can go days without milk for the kids. Forget about driving to see the kids in sports because of your need to get drunk or inability to drive since you are too drunk. For the addicted person, feeding their addiction is the only thing of importance and anyone or anything else is second priority.

Addiction is one of the highest forms of selfishness. The only thing that matters is getting that fix regardless of the consequences and who it hurts. The depth of my selfishness was brought home to me when my son once told me that if I died from smoking, it would hurt him more than it would hurt me. That statement cut to my heart, but unfortunately wasn't enough to cause me to quit. I know that is so sad. He was exactly right. I would be dead and no longer in pain, but he would be left with the heartache of my choices. Another example of my addictions being selfish is when my husband died suddenly and afterward I stayed high on pot. I was in so much pain that all I cared about was getting numb. When I was high I could retreat into my own little world. Did I stop to think about my hurting kids? Did I care that the time I spent hiding in my addiction was time taken away from them? Not enough to cause me to change.

If the addict is still living in the house, the household is affected and frustrated by their choices. We want to just slap the person upside the head, shake them, and knock some sense into their ignorant thinking. I know that sounds violent, but the emotions are strong when in a relationship with someone who is making bad choices—choices that hurt them and harm the family unit. This is where we must take responsibility for our own actions and ask God to heal our damaged and broken emotions.

Feelings of disgust arise when we see the person altered because of their addiction and wonder how anyone can behave that way. We think, "If they could only see themselves, they wouldn't do it anymore." If only that were true, we could videotape them and that would stop the addictions. Many times there is verbal and possibly even physical abuse by the addicted person and they don't even remember. You are left with mental, emotional, and physical scars and they seem to get off scot-free. It doesn't seem fair and it isn't! The addicted person does suffer, which adds to the addictions' strength because they have to numb their own feelings of disgust over what they are doing.

Chances are you have hidden the liquor, drugs, money, or cigarettes in hopes of discouraging their use. You have probably threatened but usually to no avail. You have probably prayed prayers of desperation. All these things are our ways of trying to control someone who uses no self-control. We feel so helpless that we lash out trying to control the other person and then when our plan doesn't work we feel even more helpless and hopeless.

The hardest emotion to deal with when we are in a relationship with an addict is that of rejection. We can't understand why this person who is supposed to love and take care of us is hurting us so much. Can't they see what their actions are doing to us and to them? Don't they care? Will they ever change? How can we change them? These are all normal feelings and questions, but the answer is not simple. The only control we have is our own self-control and that is not easy in these situations. Many times our lives are so out of control because of the actions of the addicted that we become addicted to trying to control the addict. We find ourselves dealing with the conflicting emotions of hatred, love, and caring. It's a catch twenty-two and an emotional roller coaster.

We must remember that no matter what, we are not responsible for another person's addiction. We are responsible for our own actions. We did not make that person become addicted and we cannot break their addiction for them, regardless of how badly it needs to be broken or how terribly it affects our life. We are not and cannot be responsible for another person's actions.

God showed me years ago that I was codependent on my husband's addiction to anger and rage. What that means is that I allowed his feelings to become my own. I tried to make him happy and was miserable if he wasn't. The control was all messed up, as his addiction became an addiction for me as I tried to change him by changing my actions. Instead of my own self-control, I was being controlled and trying to control him by what I did or didn't do. Either way is out of balance and only brings heartache and unrest. It is easy to allow someone else's behavior to devour and consume our thoughts, actions, and feelings.

> Be well balanced (temperate, sober of mind),
> be vigilant and cautious at all times; for that
> enemy of yours, the devil, roams around like a
> lion roaring [in fierce hunger], seeking someone
> to seize upon and devour.
>
> —1 PETER 5:8, AMP

When we get out of balance, we give Satan authority to devour us. Let's look at what this scripture has to say about self-control.

> But the fruit of the Spirit is love, joy, peace, longsuffering, kindness, goodness, faithfulness, gentleness, self-control. Against such there is no law. And those who are Christ's have crucified the flesh with its passions and desires.
>
> —GALATIANS 5:22–24, NKJV

We need the fruit of the Holy Spirit in our lives because it is not something we have in and of ourselves. If you have accepted Jesus as your Savior, the seed of the Holy Spirit lives in you; and just like natural fruit, seeds take time to grow. You can water your seed and fertilize it with God's Word, time with the Son, and by the power of the Holy Spirit. Begin by praying for Him to produce the fruit of self-control in your life. Did you notice that lovely word *longsuffering*? It's not one of my favorites either. These things don't come quickly or easily, but they do come as we spend time with God instead of our problem.

> And "don't sin by letting anger control you." Don't let the sun go down while you are still angry, for anger gives a foothold to the devil.
>
> —EPHESIANS 4:26–27

Then Peter came to Him and said, "Lord, how often shall my brother sin against me, and I forgive him? Up to seven times?" Jesus said to him, "I do not say to you, up to seven times, but up to seventy times seven."

—Matthew 18:21–23, nkjv

Let's pray.

Lord Jesus,

Please forgive me for trying to control someone other than myself. I struggle with self-control and need Your help. I have judged addicted people but I see that is wrong. Change me, O Lord, to be the person You have created me to be. Your word says that Your goodness leads people to true repentance, so I ask You to pour out Your goodness on _____ (fill in the blank). Open their eyes to Your salvation and grace. Cause them to desire Your freedom. Help me to stay out of Your way as You work in their life and focus on my relationship with You. This day I choose to trust You, obey You, and serve You, regardless of anyone else's choices. Please help me with this choice. Thank You for teaching me Your everlasting ways and forgiving me and _____ (fill in the blank). Not because they deserve it or I feel like it, but because You instruct me to, I choose by my will to forgive _____ (fill in the blank) for _____ (fill in the blank) so that I too may be forgiven. Thank You, Lord, for not giving up on us. I love You and praise You.

In Jesus' name I pray. Amen.

Chapter 7

SICK OF REPENTING

W E TEND TO VIEW REPENTING AS A NEGATIVE thing when in fact it is a wonderful opportunity to receive cleansing and freedom from sin. It is God's vehicle to righteousness. Repentance can be compared to Lysol, which removes odors and germs (sin stinks and causes sickness), Shout, which removes stains (sin stains our lives and consciences) Ex Lax, which removes clogged-up junk in our lives, or like milk, it does a body good.

What exactly does repentance mean? There are three Greek words used in the New Testament to denote repentance: (1) The verb, *metamelomai*, is used of a change of mind, such as to produce regret or even remorse on account of sin, but not necessarily a change of heart. This word is used with reference to the repentance of Judas in Matthew 27:3. (2) *Metanoeo*, means to change one's mind and purpose as the result of knowledge. This verb, with (3) the cognate noun, *metanoia*, is used of true repentance, a change of mind and purpose and life, to which remission of sin is promised.[1]

Evangelical repentance consists of (1) a true sense of one's own guilt and sinfulness; (2) an apprehension of God's mercy in Christ; (3) an actual hatred of sin (Ps. 119:128; Job 42:5–6; 2 Cor. 7:10) and turning from it to God; and (4) a persistent endeavor after a holy life in a walking with God in the way of His commandments. The true penitent is conscious of guilt (Ps. 51:4, 9), of pollution (51:5, 7, 10), and of helplessness (51:11; 109:21–22). Thus he apprehends himself to be just what God has always seen him to be and declares him to be. But repentance comprehends not only such a sense of sin, but also an apprehension of mercy, without which there can be no true repentance (Ps. 51:1; 130:4).[2]

The first definition given is one of a changed mind. We can begin to change our mind about repenting of our sin by confessing it as such and then asking God to forgive us. If we are talking about an addiction such as smoking, there may be a lot of confessing. But trust me; as you begin to confess it every time and ask God to help you hate the sin because it is harming you, it does help you to want to put it down. Just the fact that you are reading this book is in itself an act of repentance. You want to change your mind about your actions or you probably wouldn't be reading it. God will have to change your heart, as that is His part and which He always does. But we need to do our part, which is to repent and to renew our minds.

The evangelical definition is great because it is all-inclusive of the guilt we have before being cleansed, our change in purpose, and God's mercy. We will change from choosing death into choosing life. We must remember that whatever our addiction or perpetual sin is, it brings death to our bodies, minds, spirits, and relationships. God wants us to choose life, not death and blessings, not curses.

Today I have given you the choice between life and death, between blessings and curses. Now I call on heaven and earth to witness the choice you make. Oh, that you would choose life, so that you and your descendants might live!

—DEUTERONOMY 30:19, NLT

The key is simply turning from our sin (before, during, or even after) to God for His deliverance, forgiveness, and strength for deliverance from the sin that has hold of us.

Many times we get sick of saying the same thing over and over again and may feel like a hypocrite. A hypocrite is someone who pretends to be what he or she is not. We can know what we are doing isn't good or right and yet still do it. This doesn't make us a hypocrite, just a human who is still learning to appropriate God's truth into our life. If we go around condemning others with addictions and acting holier than them, then we *are* hypocrites and being judgmental. If we are pretending, we must repent of that. Another trap we may fall into is in thinking that confessing and repenting are useless because nothing seems to be changing. That's where our faith comes in. We confess and repent because God says to.

Faith is the confidence that what we hope for will actually happen; it gives us assurance about things we cannot see.

—HEBREWS 11:1

With each act of faith and obedience, we come closer to God and our hope increases. We are turning from darkness to light, from death to life, and from addiction to self or self-gratification to selflessness. Our focus gets turned to where it should be, on our almighty, all-powerful Lord instead of on our faults, failures, and frailties.

> For the Lord is the Spirit, and wherever the Spirit of the Lord is, there is freedom.
>
> —2 CORINTHIANS 3:17

This book and our relationship with God is all about freedom—freedom from any ruling power in our lives including death and eternal separation from our Lord. Who wouldn't want that? Satan!! Remember that Satan is our enemy and will use any and every trick he can to keep us in the prison of addiction. God makes things simple for us; Satan muddies the waters.

This works! For me it has been a process over a period of years, but for you it may only be a day, a week, or a month. We sometimes think that this problem we have had for ten years should be gone in a week. Sometimes that happens, but usually it takes longer. Just don't give up!

> Do not be terrified by them, for the LORD your God, who is among you, is a great and awesome God. The LORD your God will drive out those nations before you, little by little. You will not be allowed to eliminate them all at once, or the wild animals will multiply around you. But the

Lord your God will deliver them over to you, throwing them into great confusion until they are destroyed.

—Deuteronomy 7:21–23, niv

If you are like me, you are or have struggled with several addictions simultaneously. Also, you want everything done now. This is a problem for an addict because when that doesn't happen, we get defeated and give up. It's the all or nothing mentality. Be patient and only deal with the thing God has you dealing with right now. I know the above scripture is referring to a nation or a place, but the principal can be applied to places in our souls as well. God will deliver and help us a little at a time, one step and one day at a time, according to His plan, not ours.

For I know the thoughts and plans that I have for you, says the Lord, thoughts and plans for welfare and peace and not for evil, to give you hope in your final outcome.

—Jeremiah 29:11, amp

Let's look at what scriptures say about confessing our sin and repentance.

If we confess our sins, He is faithful and just to forgive us our sins and to cleanse us from all unrighteousness.

—1 John 1:9, nkjv

Our part is to confess our sin. When we do that, His part is to forgive us and cleanse us of all unrighteousness. Where else can we get that kind of a deal? Sometimes we think it's just too hard or is a waste of time; but I am here to tell you, just as we read, Jesus is faithful regardless of our faithfulness.

> Confess your sins to each other and pray for each other so that you may be healed. The earnest prayer of a righteous person has great power and produces wonderful results.
>
> —JAMES 5:16

Find someone you can confess to in confidentiality. When we are held accountable, it helps us to not be so quick to jump into sin, knowing that we will have to own up to our actions. AA uses this type of accountability to help their members refrain from drinking. Weight Watchers uses group meetings to help ward off those late night binges. There is something about having another human, someone we can touch and see, knowing our business that helps keep us in line. Even though God knows and sees everything we do, since we can't physically touch or see Him, we may be deluded into thinking we are getting away with something.

Sometimes we don't want to confess our sin because we really aren't ready to give it up. If that's where you are, that's where you start the confession process. Start by admitting that you like your addiction, even though it's hurting you and others, and ask God to give you eyes to see its true destruction. Ask Him to give you hatred for whatever it is that is controlling you so that you can desire the freedom to break from it. Ask Him for a vision and taste of freedom so that the desire for freedom outweighs the desire for the bondage.

I remember liking, even loving, my addiction to pot and cigarettes. I still have to be careful not to get back into that wrong train of thinking that I am missing out on something. I love being free. Even though the road wasn't always lovely, it was worth every step, slip, blunder, and mistake it took to get there.

I had to start confessing my addictions as idolatry. That's right, idolatry. It was my god; what I bowed down to; what took my time, attention, and money, which all belong to the true living God.

> I am the LORD your God, who rescued you from the land of Egypt, the place of your slavery. You must not have any other god but me. You must not make for yourself an idol of any kind or an image of anything in the heavens or on the earth or in the sea. You must not bow down to them or worship them, for I, the LORD your God, am a jealous God who will not tolerate your affection for any other gods. I lay the sins of the parents upon their children; the entire family is affected—even children in the third and fourth generations of those who reject me. But I lavish unfailing love for a thousand generations on those who love me and obey my commands.
>
> —EXODUS 20:2–6

We start where we are. One of the things that helped me desire to repent and be free was to visualize a single cigarette, a pack of cigarettes, a joint, or whatever in front of me, and then me bowing down to it in worship. I know that sounds ridiculous, but in all reality, that is exactly what we are doing. We carry our little god around with us. When our flesh cries in pain for the nicotine or the high, we bow down again and run to satisfy that craving or urge. Use your imagination in a good way. See your addiction with little arms and legs attached to it talking to you and beckoning you to bow down to it. This sounds crazy but when we see and admit that we are allowing it to dictate and destroy our lives, repentance is so much easier.

Have you ever thought of an inanimate object being ruler over your life? Imagine a beer bottle with arms and legs making you its servant. How about a candy bar commanding you to drop to your knees and shove him in your mouth? This is exactly what we do when we allow these external factors to control us. It is easier to ask forgiveness for giving power and control over to such a small god when we have such a huge God on our side. Surely the God who created the whole earth, holds it together, causes everything to fit together, and knows everything about us can equip us to walk away from our addiction.

> ...for through him God created everything in the heavenly realms and on earth. He made the things we can see and the things we can't see—such as thrones, kingdoms, rulers, and authorities in the unseen world. Everything

was created through him and for him. He
existed before anything else, and he holds all
creation together.

—Colossians 1:16–17

I am using these examples not to condemn anyone, but
because they helped me do my part, which is to confess my
sin and turn from it to God.

So now there is no condemnation for those
who belong to Christ Jesus. And because you
belong to him, the power of the life-giving
Spirit has freed you from the power of sin that
leads to death.

—Romans 8:1–2

Remember that you have an enemy, Satan, who wants to
kill, steal, and destroy you. He will do whatever he can to
make you give up and stay in your prison cell of addiction,
guilt, condemnation, and defeat so that you are useless and
consumed with nothing but your addiction. God reminds us
not to give up and to keep our minds focused and transformed by His Word.

For he who sows to his flesh will of the flesh
reap corruption, but he who sows to the Spirit
will of the Spirit reap everlasting life. And
let us not grow weary while doing good, for
in due season we shall reap if we do not lose
heart. Therefore, as we have opportunity, let us

do good to all, especially to those who are of
the household of faith.

—GALATIANS 6:8–10, NKJV

Repenting is simply confessing our sin, turning from
it to God, and asking for His help. It is easy to get sick of
doing the same thing over and over again, but remember,
that's what we are doing with our addiction. We just need
to change the focus of our addiction to something that will
bring eventual freedom. It may feel foolish to confess a sin
maybe even a thousand times and see no results. But our
responsibility is to turn to God and to trust Him for the
results, not ourselves. We are sowing to the Spirit when we
pray and focus on God. We are sowing to our flesh when we
give into our addiction. When we pray, let's remember to ask
God to help us not to lose heart.

> Then Peter came to Him and said, "Lord, how
> often shall my brother sin against me, and I
> forgive him? Up to seven times?" Jesus said to
> him, "I do not say to you, up to seven times, but
> up to seventy times seven."

—MATTHEW 18:21–22, NKJV

Now if God wants us, who are imperfect, to forgive that
much, how much more will He, who *is* perfect, forgive us
when we fail? There is a line in the book *The Shack*, which
says "I don't need to punish people for sin. Sin is its own
punishment. It's not my purpose to punish it, it's my joy to
cure it."[3]

Let's pray together now.

Lord Jesus,

I confess my sin of _____ (fill in the blank). I change my mind about trying to hide this thing from you. I acknowledge that only You can help me. You will show and are showing me what to do. I repent of disobeying and giving up and doing things my way instead of Yours. Please help me, Lord. I ask that You forgive me for idolatry, bowing down to the god of _____ (fill in the blank with all that applies). I want You to be my one and only God from this day forward. Lord, I ask that You help me not give up on repenting, believing, and confessing no matter how many times I must do it. You are patient and kind and will not turn Your back on me. Thank You for that promise. I ask that You forgive me for giving up on myself, on You, and on hope. I forgive myself for my failures and ask that You restore me to health. I forgive You, even though You are perfect and need no forgiveness, because I feel as if You require me to do and be things I can't. Forgive me for this wrong thinking. You have freed me from the law because I can't keep it even though I continue to try. Clean the slate of wrong thinking today, Lord. I receive Your forgiveness as I continue to confess my sin and believe that I will be free.

In Jesus' name I pray. Amen.

Chapter 8

HELP! I'VE FALLEN AND I CAN'T GET UP

So, what do you think? With God on our side like this, how can we lose? If God didn't hesitate to put everything on the line for us, embracing our condition and exposing himself to the worst by sending his own Son, is there anything else he wouldn't gladly and freely do for us? And who would dare tangle with God by messing with one of God's chosen? Who would dare even to point a finger? The One who died for us—who was raised to life for us!—is in the presence of God at this very moment sticking up for us. Do you think anyone is going to be able to drive a wedge between us and Christ's love for us? There is no way! Not trouble, not hard times, not hatred, not hunger, not homelessness, not bullying threats, not backstabbing, not even the worst sins listed in scripture:... None of this fazes us because Jesus loves us. I'm absolutely convinced that nothing—nothing living or dead, angelic or demonic, today or tomorrow, high or low, thinkable or unthinkable—absolutely nothing can get between us and God's love because of the way that Jesus our Master has embraced us.
—ROMANS 8:31–39,
THE MESSAGE, EMPHASIS ADDED

THIS PLAINLY LETS US KNOW THAT NOTHING, ADDICtions included, can separate us from His love. He won't give up on us, so who are we to give up on ourselves.

These scriptures are not listed as a license to stay in our sins but as motivation to get out of them.

> For the wages of sin is death, but the gift of God is eternal life in Christ Jesus our Lord.
>
> —ROMANS 6:23, NKJV

We are beginning to see that God knows that we will have trials and tribulations yet He will provide a way out for us. We are not alone in our struggles.

> But where sin abounded, grace abounded much more.
>
> —ROMANS 5:20, NKJV

We cannot out-sin God's grace, so never give up on God, His forgiveness, or His help, which is the only thing that will bring us to true victory.

WHY HAVE I FALLEN BACK INTO THIS MESS AGAIN?

> As a dog returns to his own vomit, so a fool repeats his folly.
>
> —PROVERBS 26:11, NKJV

Ouch, that's strong! It is so gross to see a dog lick its vomit. Think about it. Vomit is putrid stuff we expel from our body. You may be thinking, "I don't go back and lick my vomit." But when we put the garbage back into our bodies that we have been freed from, whether it is cigarettes, drugs, alcohol, or any other addictive substance, it is like returning to and enjoying our vomit. When we go back to or give into sexual sins and impure thoughts, we are returning to the vomit of guilt and shame.

Webster defines *fool* as a person with little or no judgment, common sense, or wisdom.[1] This is where we need to go to God, to confess our sins as many times as it takes, and to ask Him for wisdom.

James 1:5 (NKJV) says:

> If any of you lacks wisdom, let him ask of God,
> who gives to all liberally and without reproach,
> and it will be given to him.

What is *folly*? Webster's tells us it is a lack of understanding, sense, or radical conduct; foolishness or any foolish and useless but expensive undertaking or action that ends or can end in disaster.[2] Again, ouch! This seems harsh to me, but we have to see our actions and behaviors for what they are. They are harmful. They are expensive, costing us our health, money, time, and relationships. These things are not being said to condemn us but to lead us to a full desire to be free from our vomit.

How much sense does it make to keep smoking, drinking, or doing drugs, knowing it will eventually destroy our health and appearance and our finances? How many times will we continue in this behavior before we seek wisdom and understanding and say, "I have allowed this thing to control me long enough"? We can know that what we are doing is wrong. We can hate it before, during, and after we submit to the addiction but that doesn't seem to be enough to stop us, does it? What needs to change? How can we change these negative feelings of guilt and finally break free from destructive patterns and behaviors?

Patiently read and reread what Paul wrote about these same feelings of discouragement over the same habitual sins:

> So, since we're out from under the old tyranny, does that mean we can live any old way we want? Since we're free in the freedom of God, can we do anything that comes to mind? Hardly. You know well enough from your own experience that there are some acts of so-called freedom that destroy freedom. Offer yourselves to sin, for instance, and it's your last free act. But offer yourselves to the ways of God and the freedom never quits. All your lives you've let sin tell you what to do. But thank God you've started listening to a new master, one whose commands set you free to live openly in his freedom!
>
> —ROMANS 6:15, THE MESSAGE

I'm using this freedom language because it's easy to picture. You can readily recall, can't you, how at one time the more you did just what you felt like doing—not caring about others, not caring about God—the worse your life became and the less freedom you had? And how much different is it now as you live in God's freedom, your lives healed and expansive in holiness? As long as you did what you felt like doing, ignoring God, you didn't have to bother with right thinking or right living, or right anything for that matter. But do you call that a free life? What did you get out of it? Nothing you're proud of now. Where did it get you? A dead end. But now that you've found you don't have to listen to sin tell you what to do, and have discovered the delight of listening to God telling you, what a surprise! A whole, healed, put-together life right now, with more and more of life on the way! Work hard for sin your whole life and your pension is death. But God's gift is real life, eternal life, delivered by Jesus, our Master.

—ROMANS 6:19–23, THE MESSAGE

I can anticipate the response that is coming: "I know that all God's commands are spiritual, but I'm not. Isn't this also your experience?" Yes. I'm full of myself—after all, I've spent a long time in sin's prison. What I don't understand about myself is that I decide one way, but then I act another, doing things I absolutely despise. So if I can't be trusted to figure out what is best for myself and then do it, it becomes obvious that God's command is necessary.

—ROMANS 7:14, THE MESSAGE

But I need something more! For if I know the law but still can't keep it, and if the power of sin within me keeps sabotaging my best intentions, I obviously need help! I realize that I don't have what it takes. I can will it, but I can't do it. I decide to do good, but I don't really do it; I decide not to do bad, but then I do it anyway. My decisions, such as they are, don't result in actions. Something has gone wrong deep within me and gets the better of me every time.

—ROMANS 7:17, THE MESSAGE

It happens so regularly that it's predictable. The moment I decide to do good, sin is there to trip me up. I truly delight in God's commands, but it's pretty obvious that not all of me joins in that delight. Parts of me covertly rebel, and just when I least expect it, they take charge....I've tried everything and nothing helps. I'm at the end of my rope. Is there no one who can do anything for me? Isn't that the real question? The answer, thank God, is that Jesus Christ can and does. He acted to set things right in this life of contradictions where I want to serve God with all my heart and mind, but am pulled by the influence of sin to do something totally different.

—ROMANS 7:21, 24–25, THE MESSAGE

I love the realness of these scriptures. Even Paul is saying, "Hey, I know what I am doing is wrong, I decide not to it (whatever your particular it is) but then I go and still do it. What am I to do? How am I supposed to ever get free? Why do I keep coming back to the same old dead end?" According to the above scriptures and my experience, the good news is that even though we can't break free in and of ourselves, through the power of Jesus Christ, we can and will!

We need to change our thinking and see ourselves as not in jail but free. Yes, even right in the middle of our mess. We can begin to confess our sin for what it is—life stealing and damaging. We can confess our inability to deal with this monster. We can go to God every second of every day, asking for His help, strength, mercy, grace, and desires.

…apart from me you can do nothing.

—JOHN 15:5

I know that *sounds* easy, doesn't it? Also, when we don't see instant results our first temptation is to give up and say this doesn't work. Guess what? That's a lie! God's Word is true regardless of our feelings or circumstances. When we are in any addictive habit and we give into the temptation, it brings a certain instant result of satisfaction. We therefore want that instant satisfaction of being free from it, but generally speaking, that doesn't happen. We can take each instance of temptation, each time we fall, to the throne room of grace, Jesus, and pray to be freed once again from the power and entanglement of sin. We can and need to ask God to make a way out for us and He will.

> No temptation has overtaken you except such as is common to man; but God is faithful, who will not allow you to be tempted beyond what you are able, but with the temptation will also make the way of escape, that you may be able to bear it.
>
> —1 CORINTHIANS 10:13–14, NKJV

Before we experience freedom, there may be a time or season where we continue in the addiction by succumbing to urges. Don't use this as a time to give up. This is the perfect opportunity to stay close to our Heavenly Father for His love and assurance and power. We have seen through scripture that we can't earn or deserve His love or grace, that we can't make Him not love us regardless of our actions, and that He won't give up on us.

Please be encouraged that if you are still active in giving into your addiction, begin to pray for God's deliverance. Pray for His strength and wisdom to cause you to desire freedom more than you desire the satisfaction of giving in to the addiction. Ask Him to help you see the benefits of freedom as opposed to the tragedy of bondage. You can ask Jesus to help you out of your self-made dungeon and pit of despair. He is our Helper and Comforter, and He is pleased, not mad, when we go to Him for help, regardless of how many times a day.

Father,

Forgive me for falling back into the sin You have delivered me from. I need Your wisdom and grace once again. Thank You for not turning Your back on me when I need You most. Just as You delivered the Israelites when they turned to You, I know You will be faithful to deliver me as well. I can't do this on my own but I know I can do all things through Christ who strengthens me. Thank You, Lord, that You are faithful and just and deliver me and cleanse me of all unrighteousness. I need Your way of thinking and godly wisdom so I will come to my senses and flee from this sin which so easily entangles me. Thank You, my God, for being my helper, deliverer, strong tower, righteousness, and the lover of my soul.

In Jesus' name I pray and believe. Amen!

Chapter 9

OBSESSIVE THINKING

I BELIEVE THAT OBSESSIVE THINKING AND ADDICTIONS go hand in hand. Your addiction may be obsessive thinking or obsessively thinking about your addiction. Either way it's controlling and unhealthy. How many times do you catch yourself thinking of your addiction or about quitting your addiction? It's almost always, whether you are full blown in the middle of it or just starting to quit or almost there, it is mind consuming.

Regardless of what the thought is about, whether it is addictions, a person, lack of a person, a substance, a place, or what you do or don't have, it consumes almost every waking hour, even during prayer. It's like a low, soft hum continuously in my head that I can't seem to shake. Why do we get things stuck in our head that just won't go away? How do we get rid of these thoughts? Is it even possible? We will explore the answers in this chapter.

Your obsessive thinking may be about your children and their future or choices, your home, your partner or the lack thereof. Maybe you're thinking of your addiction, your body appearance, food, sex, drugs or alcohol, or even an offense committed years ago or recently. Regardless of what the theme of your thoughts is, it is and can be all consuming.

When I get something in my head, it is so hard to shake. It seems like if I am thinking about it, I am praying to get rid of it. If I am not thinking about or praying about it, I realize I am not and the whole cycle starts again. Is it addictive? I would say yes. Can it be conquered? Absolutely! Will it be the last time I have to deal with this way of thinking? Probably not, but it does get less frequent and easier to deal with once you learn how to change your thinking or the object of your thoughts. I think it starts with something we want, think we have to have, or something we deserve. It is rooted in discontentment. Most times it's over what we don't have or can't have.

Let me use an example from my life. There is a man I met to whom I was attracted. I prayed every day about this man and a relationship with him. I kept being drawn to him in spite of not wanting a relationship at the time. I didn't know if I should run or stay with him. I kept telling myself that God orders our steps when we ask Him, but I kept wondering if I was hearing correctly from the Lord, so I prayed about that as well. I found myself obsessing over where this man was and what he was doing. Would he call and if so when, would he want to see me as much as I wanted to see him, was he lying to me about everything, and was he the one for me? I was constantly carrying the phone around with me in hopes that he would call or checking my email to see if he sent a note. When he did call or write, I found myself being disappointed because the conversation wasn't as long as I would have liked or about what I think it should have been about. I was in constant turmoil about what the future held, if anything. I felt like I wanted to devour this man and have him all to myself.

Does any of this sound familiar? What is your obsessive thinking about? Do you find your mind always returning to the same type of thinking? Are your expectations met when and if you get some sort of action or reaction? Are you left with a large hole of unmet expectations? I know I am. No matter what happens or doesn't happen, it is never enough or right. Why is that? Because we have grandiose ideas and desires that are unreal expectations. We haven't learned to rest and trust and be thankful with what we have and where we are in life.

Yes, we are greedy and perfectionistic in our thought life so therefore there is never going to be satisfaction, which leaves us feeling even emptier and in despair. That puts us in panic mode and then we begin to try to make things happen, whether we do this intentionally or not. If it's a guy, we start making the calls, sending the emails, or giving compliments in hope of snagging and capturing this thing we think we have to have to be happy. When these tactics don't work, we then must begin to scheme to find more productive ways of enticing our latest obsession. As we know, this leads to more obsession, more disappointment, and feelings of despair and hopelessness. So what's the answer? How do we break this cycle of obsessive thinking?

The mind is a very powerful instrument that must be reprogrammed. We may think that we have no control over our thoughts, but we do. We can control what we dwell on, what stays and what goes. There are at least three scriptures that teach us what to think about as well as what to do with the thoughts that pop in our minds.

> And now, dear brothers and sisters, one final thing. Fix your thoughts on what is true, and honorable, and right, and pure, and lovely, and admirable. Think about things that are excellent and worthy of praise. Keep putting into practice all you learned and received from me—everything you heard from me and saw me doing. Then the God of peace will be with you.
>
> —PHILIPPIANS 4:8–9

> For the weapons of our warfare are not carnal but mighty in God for pulling down strongholds, casting down arguments and every high thing that exalts itself against the knowledge of God, bringing every thought into captivity to the obedience of Christ.
>
> —2 CORINTHIANS 10:4–5, NKJV

> …but be transformed by the renewing of your mind, that you may prove what is that good and acceptable and perfect will of God.
>
> —ROMANS 12:2, NKJV

We can see that we are to think about what is good, we are to bring negative, obsessive thoughts to Jesus, and we are to renew our minds with God's Word so we know what His will is.

As with anything else in life that is worth having, it takes patience and discipline. I know these are difficult words for the obsessive thinker or addict because we want everything now and we want it right (or the way we think it should be). Sorry to burst your bubble.

As I have struggled with obsessive thought patterns, God has graciously shown me some things motivating these thoughts. One of the things I have been shown is greed, which is simply wanting more than what you have. Greed is being discontent with what you have or don't have, no matter how good it is. Another thing is pride—thinking you deserve it all or more. And finally, wrong expectations—expecting things to be one way and when they aren't, becoming preoccupied with the results.

Each one of these is deadly to our emotions, peace, and state of mind. It was greed that caused me to want more of this man's time than he was able or even wanting to give. Then I was discontent because my desires of him were not being met. Instead of being thankful for the relationship and friendship that I had, I was being greedy, wanting more. I wanted *all* of his time and attention and for him to lay his life down for me to be at my every beck and call. And I wanted him to be just as obsessed with me as I was with him. Can you see the pride in all those desires? It's ugly and harmful, isn't it? The sad but true thing is that if those desires had been fulfilled, it probably would have sickened me and I would have run away as fast as I could.

When we don't get what we want or refuse to be thankful for what we have, discontentment is right there screaming at us, "How can you be satisfied with this? You know there's more and you don't have it! Are you going to rest or fight for what you want?" When we then try to fight for what we want, we are still left empty. If we have to fight for it, we are still going to be discontent when we get it. It will not meet our expectations and so we need to look at something else to go after. Same cycle, different day.

When I conveyed my expectations to my friend about wanting more time and he was very clear that his time is quite consumed, did that change my expectations? *No!* Did it make me want it more? Yes! Is it his fault that my expectations are not met? I would love to be able to say yes, because that would relieve me of my own personal responsibility for contentment and placing that impossible job onto someone else. When we look to someone or something else for our contentment, we will always be disappointed because people cannot meet those needs we have. Until we realize this dangerous pattern of thinking, we will continue to look to others for our well being, which is an addictive pattern.

What addiction do you know of not rooted in greed? I can't think of any because an addict is striving to relive a momentary state of comfort that all too often evades us. We can't have just one puff, one drink, one hit, one wager, one piece of dessert or sexual satisfaction. We want more and more and more because we are not satisfied. We are only masking a much deeper need for fulfillment.

Not that I speak in regard to need, for I have learned in whatever state I am, to be content.

—PHILIPPIANS 4:11, NKJV

We expect that whatever we are obsessing over will meet our needs once it is obtained. Does it? No! Once we are left with that disappointment, we obsess over that as well. What can I do to change things or to make them happen? What do I need to do differently? When we have expectations of ourselves or others, communication is the key. Being honest with ourselves, anyone else involved, and most importantly with the Lord is a must. We need to communicate our expectations to others, which is our responsibility.

Now when our expectation isn't met, we must not be unrealistic in obsessing over it changing. It's the unrealistic thinking that leads to discontent because we are not content with the truth that we expecting. We have two choices at this point; we can accept what is available or decide we don't want to settle for the answer and move on. We cannot force someone to comply with our every need and demand. It may work for awhile but in reality, it only prolongs the pain because people will disappoint us. It's a way of life. This is said not to bring hopelessness but to face a reality. God is the only one that can bring true contentment when we place our trust in Him for our needs and desires. Sometimes our need is to simply learn to do without something or someone and find true joy and happiness and contentment in our Lord.

As for God, His way is perfect; The word of the LORD is proven; He is a shield to all who trust in Him.

—PSALM 18:30, NKJV

Once this is accomplished, we are steady, sure, and immovable regarding our situation, circumstance, and desires. Then we *know* our needs will be met, and we begin to trade our expectations for those of our Lord Jesus Christ. How do we get to this point?

Let me give you another example of obsessive thinking that God has brought me through. My husband died a little over a year ago and, needless to say, it left me completely shocked and in turmoil over my future. Like many married couples, we planned our lives and future together. We had hopes and dreams about retirement, college for the kids, and futures for ourselves. When he died, our plans for the future died. My expectations for the future died. Everything changed that day and the days that followed. I was one of the blessed widows who had life insurance to pay our bills and give me a cushion for the future. You would think that that would be enough to sustain me, but I obsessed over my future. What was I going to do to support myself? Out of obedience to where I felt God had called me, I was a lunch lady in a high school so that wasn't an option to supporting me, my two kids, and our lifestyle. I am in my early forties with no training to speak of, so I couldn't rely on my education or work experience for support. I knew I was OK for a couple of years, but then what?

I remember being obsessed about spending and wondering

what I would do when the money ran out. It was almost crippling. When these thoughts came, by faith I would say aloud, "God, I trust You." I didn't feel it. I didn't even know that I truly believed it, but I would confess it and ask God to help my unbelief. Through a series of events, such as praying, staying in God's Word, and spending lots of time allowing God to love me, He did assure me of His unconditional love and provision for me.

> And my God shall supply all your need according
> to His riches in glory by Christ Jesus.
>
> —Philippians 4:19, nkjv

I awoke one morning with the same song playing in my head, "What are you going to do? How will you make it? Are you going to be homeless?" God showed me that even though my circumstances had changed; He never changes and is always the same, today, yesterday, and forevermore (Heb. 13:7). Even though the source God used as my provision (my husband's income) had changed, He is the true provider of finances and life. Although my expectations for my future changed, His plans for me remained unchanged.

> I'll show up and take care of you as I promised
> and bring you back home. I know what I'm
> doing. I have it all planned out—plans to take
> care of you, not abandon you, plans to give you
> the future you hope for.
>
> —Jeremiah 29:11, The Message

All my hopes and dreams involved things that are never guaranteed and will not fail to change. That's when I realized that my focus and trust were in the wrong place and on the wrong things. I had to renew my mind (Rom. 12:1). I had to continue to learn how to bring my thoughts captive to Jesus.

> For the weapons of our warfare are not carnal but mighty in God for pulling down strongholds, casting down arguments and every high thing that exalts itself against the knowledge of God, bringing every thought into captivity to the obedience of Christ, and being ready to punish all disobedience when your obedience is fulfilled.
>
> —2 CORINTHIANS 10:4–6, NKJV

This simply means bringing the thoughts you are thinking to Jesus as they pop in your head. It takes time and practice, but it is doable. When I would think, "I am going to do without," I had to remind myself of what God says, which is that He will supply all my needs. When I thought, "What can I do at my age?" I had to remind myself of what He says, which is I can do all things through Christ who strengthens me. When I wondered how I would support my family, I was reminded that God is my supplier, therefore theirs as well. When loneliness came and the thoughts of how I was all alone, I again was reminded that He will never leave me nor forsake me.

> Because he has set his love upon Me, therefore will I deliver him; I will set him on high,

because he knows and understands My name [has a personal knowledge of My mercy, love, and kindness—trusts and relies on Me, knowing I will never forsake him, no, never].

—Psalm 91:14

Let your character or moral disposition be free from love of money [including greed, avarice, lust, and craving for earthly possessions] and be satisfied with your present [circumstances and with what you have]; for He [God] Himself has said, I will not in any way fail you nor give you up nor leave you without support. [I will] not, [I will] not, [I will] not in any degree leave you helpless nor forsake nor let [you] down (relax My hold on you)! [Assuredly not!]

—Hebrews 13:5, amp

Of course if you don't know what scripture says, you can't replace those thoughts. To begin replacing these thoughts with God's thoughts, His Word, you may need to purchase a promise book. There are some awesome promise books with headings on topics of common struggles. That would be an ideal place to start to see what God promises for His children. This is not a magic formula, a quick fix, a band-aid, or even an easy fix. It is a process which will bring healing for eternity. This process may not be easy and definitely takes time, but it is worth every second because you get the honor of being in God's presence. In God's presence is fullness of joy.

> You will show me the path of life; in Your pres-
> ence is fullness of joy, at Your right hand there
> are pleasures forevermore.
>
> —PSALM 16:11, NKJV

I want to add that there is great power in our words. It is hard to speak out loud contrary to what you are thinking but that is where you need to start. When I would think about whatever the particular obsession was, I would speak out loud, "God will withhold no good thing from me." (See Psalm 84:11.) What if my obsession is not the right thing for me? God is protecting me from myself. He knows the beginning from the end, so I have no need to fear that He will keep something good from me or give me something that is not good for me. When your obsessive thinking begins, immediately begin *speaking* God's promises.

> So then faith comes by hearing, and hearing by
> the word of God.
>
> —ROMANS 10:17, NKJV

This may seem silly at first and hard to get used to but we need to hear God's Word.

Fear is almost always involved in obsessive thinking as well. It usually starts with that worry sentence, What if....? We are afraid of not having our needs met. We fear things will fall apart without our control. We think we know what's best for not only our lives but also the lives of others. God is all knowing, all powerful, and willing and able to care for us and other people. For you it may be your children, family, friends, or business associates. The truth is, God not only has our back but He is capable of taking care of the universe. We can cast our care onto Him.

> So humble yourselves under the mighty power
> of God, and at the right time he will lift you
> up in honor. Give all your worries and cares to
> God, for he cares about you.
>
> —1 Peter 5:6–7

A care is something we have concern about but the inability to change or control. Yes, I know we think we can control everything, but we truly have little control over anything. We have our place and responsibility, but we can't control people or their lives. We have self-control, which is probably the least-used type of control there is. Using self-control has never been my strong point, but I am learning that it will bring freedom.

Here is a good example of God not withholding any good thing from us, which is our fear and why we obsess so easily over things. I have a miniature Dachshund whom I adore. She is so cute and truly an answer to prayer and a gift from God. Our whole family loves this dog and wants good things for her. She has this habit of begging for people food. Yes, she is obsessed. I have always heard that people food is the worst thing you can feed dogs so we refuse to feed her our food. We are not trying to be mean or withhold any good thing from her, but we know what's best for her and want her to be healthy, not to mention not wanting her to vomit on the carpet. When she begs, it is the cutest and saddest thing you have ever seen. She is focused, intent, and won't give up. Isn't that how we get?

Rest and trust in knowing that God is not withholding something good from us. We must *renew* our minds with this truth versus the lie of going after things that are not good for us. Sometimes God will allow things in our life for which we have begged. But in His wisdom, He uses it to teach us that He does know best and loves us with an unfailing love. When we come to Him for our needs to be met, we can rest assured that He will add no trouble to it.

In summary, I believe that the way to freedom from obsessive thinking is by trusting God, first and foremost. First, this can be done by asking God to help us and teach us to trust Him. It sounds easy but when the rubber meets the road, it's not always easy. Remember He is patient and kind. Secondly, we must continue to do our part, which includes but is not limited to renewing our minds with His truth, speaking His truth, bringing our thoughts captive at their onset, and believing He loves us. Enjoy your freedom! It will come as you continue in your fellowship with Him.

> Now the Lord is the Spirit, and where the Spirit of the Lord is, there is freedom.
>
> —2 CORINTHIANS 3:17

Dear Lord,

Teach me to bring my thoughts captive to You. Forgive me for not trusting You to take care of me and my needs. My mind is a mess and I need Your healing. I need You to help me renew my mind with the truth of Your Word, Lord. I submit to You this day. I believe, Lord, help my unbelief.

In Jesus' holy name I pray. Amen!

Chapter 10

ADDICTED TO PEOPLES' OPINIONS

PEOPLE PLEASING IS ONE OF THE MOST HIDDEN AND difficult addictions because it is seen as such a good thing by most people, ourselves included. We are considered people pleasers when we are addicted to what others think of us. The reason this is an addiction is because our motives are to get others' approval, which is dangerous. When we place our self-worth and identity into the hands of people versus God's hands, we give them ownership of who we are. We tend to live for and believe what others say and think of us instead of relying on what God says about and to us. People pleasers are those people whom everyone loves; you just can't find anything wrong with them simply because they work so hard at pleasing everyone. That doesn't *sound* like a bad thing and certainly not an addiction that needs to be broken.

I will give you some personal examples, both positive and negative, about how others' opinions can affect us. First I will give an example of a negative effect. I have a teenage daughter that I love very much but who also tends to push my buttons to the core. If you know a teenage girl, I am sure you can relate. I try very hard to be a good mother and do what I think is best for her. We have very different personalities and seem to clash in our way of thinking and dealing with things. I think our relationship has been strained because of the recent death of her father, my husband. She, like most girls, was a daddy's girl and she could do no wrong in her father's sight. I was always the bad guy when it came to disciplining her, which didn't help our relationship.

When her father died, her world came crashing down around her and I know she felt abandoned. Naturally, this only added to the stress of our relationship. For a time, nothing I said or did was right. In her opinion, which she did not hesitate to verbalize, I was annoying and no one liked me. Talk about an ego buster! We were in counseling trying to work through the grief and obvious anger issues we both had towards one another when my counselor shared something so profound yet simple. She told me that I was looking for validation as a mother from my daughter and when I didn't receive it, it would just feed my anger and insecurities even more. Once I thought about her words, I realized she was right. It is not my daughter's place, or anyone else's for that matter, to validate me and make me feel important and right. We all desire and need to be validated, but we must look to the One who created us for that, not people.

All people have opinions. If we asked ten people their opinion about us, more than likely we would get ten different answers. This is why it is so dangerous for our own well being to allow them to be our foundation, our guide, or our measuring stick. Our emotions and self-worth are continuously changing depending on the person, day, or situation, when we allow opinions to be our gauge. There is a constant striving to be the best, look good, and say and do the right thing in order to get that never-ending fix of approval.

Because I was looking to an emotionally bruised, hurting, and immature person for my validation as a mother, I was constantly receiving the opposite of what I was seeking. The truth of the matter is that I have to do what is right and pleasing to God as a parent regardless of the reaction I receive from my daughter. That is definitely not always easy to do, but what I must do to have a steady foundation on which to base my identity.

Now let's look at the dangers of a "positive" opinion from someone shaping our identity. I met a man not long ago to whom I was attracted. This man is a salesman and I truly liked his ability to communicate. He told me wonderful things that any woman would want to hear. When he told me I was beautiful, attractive, loving, and caring, it made me feel so secure and special. I thought, "Yes, I am all of those things." The problem was that when those words stopped, I was left empty again and wondering, "What's wrong with me?" We then can go into panic mode seeking to hear those wonderful words spoken about us again so we can continue to feel good about ourselves.

Since people change, moods change, and behaviors change, our identity, security, and well-being also change if we are basing them upon someone else's opinion. We have no solid foundation when our hope, faith, and importance are being nurtured by other people's opinions. We are to be imitators of Christ and the Bible tells us that He was not always liked. He is still rejected and even hated. We also know that He was perfect and pleasing in God's sight. The good news is that for the people pleaser, as with any addiction, freedom is available and so sweet once obtained.

> The fear of human opinion disables; trusting in
> God protects you from that.
>
> —PROVERBS 29:25, THE MESSAGE

Why does it say the fear of human opinion disables? Our fear isn't of the person but of their rejection of us or their displeasure in us. If we displease someone, we then take that to mean that something is wrong with us or we are unworthy in some way. The meaning of the word *disable* is to make unable, unfit or ineffective; cripple; incapacitate.[1] The meaning for *disabled* is not in proper working order, out of commission.[2]

When we look at the true meaning of the word, we can see why God wants us free from the opinions of man. Instead of placing our trust in what man's opinion is of us, God wants our trust to be in Him and Him alone. How many times have you been disabled by what someone said to or about you? It has controlled how I see myself too many times. Looking back, I can actually see how it crippled my confidence in who God created me to be. Let's look at some more scriptures about the dangers of people pleasing and then we will look at the good news of who God says we are.

> At that time a severe famine struck the land
> of Canaan, forcing Abram to go down to

Egypt, where he lived as a foreigner. As he was approaching the border of Egypt, Abram said to his wife, Sarai, "Look, you are a very beautiful woman. When the Egyptians see you, they will say, 'This is his wife. Let's kill him; then we can have her!' So please tell them you are my sister. Then they will spare my life and treat me well because of their interest in you." And sure enough, when Abram arrived in Egypt, everyone spoke of Sarai's beauty. When the palace officials saw her, they sang her praises to Pharaoh, their king, and Sarai was taken into his palace. Then Pharaoh gave Abram many gifts because of her—sheep, goats, cattle, male and female donkeys, male and female servants, and camels. But the LORD sent terrible plagues upon Pharaoh and his household because of Sarai, Abram's wife. So Pharaoh summoned Abram and accused him sharply. "What have you done to me?" he demanded. "Why didn't you tell me she was your wife? Why did you say, 'She is my sister,' and allow me to take her as my wife? Now then, here is your wife. Take her and get out of here!" Pharaoh ordered some of his men to escort them, and he sent Abram out of the country, along with his wife and all his possessions.

—GENESIS 12:10–20

In the above scriptures, we see that Abram was afraid of Pharaoh and feared for his life. Now most of us can understand that, but let's not miss the fact that God had directed him to go there. His trust should have been in what God said and not what man could do to him. Abram's fear of man caused him to lie, almost caused Sarai to commit adultery, and caused a plague to come upon Pharaoh and his household. Usually the consequences of people pleasing are not so harsh, but they can be. Can you think of a time when trying to please someone or doing something wrong to save your own hide caused harm? Has it ever affected your health or your relationship with your family?

> I tell you, My friends, do not dread and be afraid of those who kill the body and after that have nothing more that they can do.
>
> —LUKE 12:4, AMP

I like how the Amplified Bible version adds in the word *dread* here because for so many years I struggled with fear of being attacked and killed in my home while alone. I have since learned that this is called *evil forebodings*, a form of fear that gives an eerie feeling that something bad will happen to us. I was reminded just the other day how I no longer struggle with evil forebodings. I have been able to share with my son, who confided in me of his struggles with a similar problem, how we can be freed from those evil imaginations. I hope these examples show the downfall of seeking people's approval over God's and also show the beauty and freedom of getting to know and trust God. Hang in there!

As our minds add imagination to these evil forebodings, it can be crippling and send us into a full blown panic attack. We must learn to trust God, His Word, and His goodness. Like any addiction you are trying to overcome, this doesn't automatically go away, but it does lessen, and eventual freedom does come when we don't give up. The more times we run to God and His Word, the more He shows His love to us which enables us to trust Him more than we trust our feelings or circumstances. This scripture is a good reminder of our weaponry in dealing with our thought life.

> For the weapons of our warfare *are* not carnal but mighty in God for pulling down strongholds, casting down arguments and every high thing that exalts itself against the knowledge of God, bringing every thought into captivity to the obedience of Christ.
>
> —2 CORINTHIANS 10:4–5, NKJV

God showed me this scripture to realize the scope of the addiction to people pleasing.

> Many people did believe in him, however, including some of the Jewish leaders. But they wouldn't admit it for fear that the Pharisees would expel them from the synagogue. For they loved human praise more than the praise of God.
>
> —JOHN 12:42–43

As you can see from the above passage, you are not alone nor the first one to be plagued by wanting to please man over God. We are all guilty of this sin to a certain degree, some more than others. No matter where we are, we can all come up higher. God looks at our heart and our motives on why we do things. When we ask Him to reveal to us our true motives, He will—not to condemn us but to free us from people pleasing so that we may be pleasing to Him.

Can you imagine rejecting your spouse or parent or best friend, someone who loves you and would give their life for you, because you feared someone else's rejection? That is what we do when we don't do what we know the Lord would have us do because we fear what someone might say or think of us. It should break our hearts to think of what we are doing, which will hopefully bring us to change. I know I have directly disobeyed God because of fearing what another person would think of me and have had to deal with the regret of my actions and wonder about the negative consequences of my disobedience. I have asked for forgiveness but if I could redo it, I would in a heartbeat.

Years ago, as a new Christian, I felt like God wanted me to take my Bible to a neighbor's house and tell him about Jesus. I knew this guy was a biker and did drugs, and honestly I was scared to go. I reasoned that I didn't really know how and the guy might laugh at me and would probably make fun of me to the other neighbors. Then I reasoned that it was my mind and not God telling me to do this and that He wouldn't ask inexperienced me to do such a big thing. But I knew in my heart that God wanted me to go talk to him. I am so sorry to say that I didn't go. The following week, this man was crushed under a car he was working on and was killed. I can only hope and assume that God spoke to someone else and that they were obedient. I have to live with that act of people pleasing every day. Sometimes there are serious consequences to people pleasing.

Most of the time people pleasing just keeps us running and trying harder and harder to be liked and please people who end up using us anyway. Instead we need to serve people out of love for God and with His love. First and foremost, we must do things with the motive of obeying and pleasing God, not people. Serving God brings us great rewards and protection.

> Bondservants, be obedient to those who are your masters according to the flesh, with fear and trembling, in sincerity of heart, as to Christ; not with eye service, as men-pleasers, but as bond-servants of Christ, doing the will of God from the heart, with goodwill doing service, as to the Lord, and not to men, knowing that whatever good anyone does, he will receive the same from the Lord, whether he is a slave or free.
>
> —EPHESIANS 6:5–8, NKJV

Those who live in the shelter of the Most High
    will find rest in the shadow of the Almighty.
This I declare about the LORD: He alone is my
    refuge, my place of safety; he is my God, and
    I trust him.

For he will rescue you from every trap and
  protect you from deadly disease.
He will cover you with his feathers. He will
  shelter you with his wings.
His faithful promises are your armor and
  protection.
Do not be afraid of the terrors of the night, nor
  the arrow that flies in the day.
Do not dread the disease that stalks in
  darkness, nor the disaster that strikes at
  midday.
Though a thousand fall at your side, though
  ten thousand are dying around you, these
  evils will not touch you.
Just open your eyes, and see how the wicked
  are punished.
If you make the LORD your refuge, if you make
  the Most High your shelter, no evil will
  conquer you; no plague will come near your
  home.
For he will order his angels to protect you
  wherever you go.
They will hold you up with their hands so you
  won't even hurt your foot on a stone.
You will trample upon lions and cobras; you
  will crush fierce lions and serpents under
  your feet!
The LORD says, "I will rescue those who love
  me. I will protect those who trust in my
  name. When they call on me, I will answer;

I will be with them in trouble. I will rescue
and honor them. I will reward them with a
long life and give them my salvation."

—Psalm 91:1–16

Wow! What promises we have for trusting in God! I need
to be rescued, protected, honored, and rewarded with a long
life, rest, shelter, and trust instead of fear and dread.

We see how the addiction to fear of people has affected
us in a negative way. Now we will look at the right kind of
fear, which is the fear of God. Here are some of the effects of
fearing God and their scriptures references.

The fear of the Lord:

- Causes us to become of one consent (1 Sam.
  11:7).

- Causes us to become mighty warriors (2
  Chron. 14:13–15).

- Keeps us from going to war (2 Chron. 17:10).

- Causes us to be faithful and have a loyal heart
  (2 Chron. 19:9).

- Is clean and endures forever (Ps. 19:9).

- Is taught (Ps. 34:11).

- Is the beginning of wisdom (Ps. 111:10).

- Is the beginning of knowledge (Prov. 1:7).

- Is chosen (Prov. 1:29).

- Causes us to hate evil (Prov. 8:13).

- Prolongs our days (Prov. 10:27).

- Gives us strong confidence (Prov. 14:26).

- Is a fountain of life, to turn one away from the snares of death (Prov. 14:27).

- Gives us the ability to depart from evil (Prov. 16:6).

- Leads to life and causes us to abide in satisfaction (Prov. 19:23).

- Leads to riches, honor, and life (Prov. 22:4).

- Is our treasure (Isa. 33:6).

- Leads to prosperity (Acts 9:31).

Chapter 11

WHAT DOES IT TAKE TO BE FREE?

WE HAVE BEEN READING ABOUT DIFFERENT addictions and their effects. Now let's get into what it takes to be free. Remember, we had to work to get into and stay in our addiction so, likewise, we will have to work to be freed from it. There is supernatural deliverance, which I have experienced. God is sovereign and can do whatever He wills and sometimes He will deliver us instantaneously. This simply means that your cravings will disappear and you will no longer be pulled towards your addiction. You don't desire or crave that addiction and are able to walk away from it. I have experienced that supernatural deliverance but have also fallen back into the same addiction. Therefore, I had to walk it out again. My prayer is that God will bring deliverance to us in whatever way will not only free us but also keep us free from our addiction.

Just as soldiers go into a war zone, we are entering a war zone. Our enemy will not necessarily just bow down to us because we want freedom. He has his agenda to destroy us.

The thief comes only to steal and kill and
destroy; I have come that they may have life,
and have it to the full.

—JOHN 10:10, NIV

When we are in a war, we need weapons, training, and
courage. There is a time of training and preparation and of
learning about the enemy.

For we do not wrestle against flesh and blood,
but against principalities, against powers,
against the rulers of the darkness of this age,
against spiritual hosts of wickedness in the
heavenly places.

—EPHESIANS 6:12, NKJV

Our war manual needs to be God's Word, the Bible. I
would encourage you to read a recent translation like *The
Message* or the *New Living Translation*. These are easy to
read and understand, especially if you are just starting to read
the Bible. I use all types of versions because they all speak
to me and give me different perspectives. Just use whichever
version makes sense to you.

Have we taken time to count the cost of our addiction?
What has it cost us and our family and loved ones? Are we
prepared for the battle that will ensue? These are questions
we must ask ourselves. Defeat is certain if we are not totally
committed to fighting and winning this war. We may suffer
casualties but this in no way means we will lose. We just
need to face this fact so we are not blindsided if or when we

fall. We can lose a battle but still win the war. This book will encourage us to not give up, no matter how many battles we may lose.

We are victorious by the words of our testimony and the Blood of the Lamb. (See Revelation 12:11.) That means because of Jesus' death, He has made it possible. We need to then learn to have our words line up with the power of God's Word. We must stop thinking and saying in our old way, such as, "This is too hard. I can't do this. I will fail again. Everyone in my family is like this so why should there be any hope for me?" The enemy of our soul will use any and every trick he can to keep us in any sin with which he has spent generations entangling us. We must stand strong and stand firm on God's Word. And when we fail, we will decide to not just lay there and die. We will get up, shake ourselves off, ask again for grace and help, and keep going.

> We can rejoice, too, when we run into problems and trials, for we know that they help us develop endurance. And endurance develops strength of character, and character strengthens our confident hope of salvation. And this hope will not lead to disappointment. For we know how dearly God loves us, because he has given us the Holy Spirit to fill our hearts with his love.
>
> —ROMANS 5:3–5

I want to state very strongly that we are in a war for our freedom, but we are not alone as soldiers. We have a commanding officer and His name is Jesus Christ—God

Himself in human form. He came and died that we may receive forgiveness and freedom from our sins. Apart from Him we can do nothing. From the minute we get up, all throughout our day, and until we go to bed, we need to be in communication with our Commander. We do this by prayer, praise, thankfulness, and by spending time in His Word.

Let's look at some of the things we will need to do to be prepared. Some of the action words used in dealing with sin are very strong such as *flee, resist, put away, throw off, surrender, confess*, and *repent*. We have our part and God has His. We can't do God's part and He won't do ours. Our relationship with God is a partnership. Salvation is free and offered to anyone, but our part is to believe and receive it. God will not override our free will. We can use our will to decide to stay in addiction or use it to be free from it; but it is our choice. We must make this choice daily, hourly, even minute by minute about whom we will serve, God or our flesh. Choose life not death.

> I call heaven and earth as witnesses today against
> you, that I have set before you life and death,
> blessing and cursing; therefore choose life, that
> both you and your descendants may live.
>
> —DEUTERONOMY 30:19, NKJV

We will break down some of the things we need to do, maybe a hundred or a thousand times a day in the beginning. Don't get overwhelmed! We are giving ourselves over to repetitive choices now with no victory; so have confidence that by making different and better choices, it will lead to freedom instead of defeat.

> Ask, and it will be given to you; seek, and you will find; knock, and it will be opened to you. For everyone who asks receives, and he who seeks finds, and to him who knocks it will be opened.
>
> —MATTHEW 7:7–8, NKJV

Our part is to ask, seek, and knock. Then the promise is that we will receive, find, and have a door opened. Does this mean that we ask, seek and knock only once and it is a done deal? Not necessarily. First, we must ask for forgiveness for our sin and freedom and deliverance from it. We ask God for the desire and strength we will need to overcome these learned and ingrained habits. Just as we developed this habit we are trying to break, we are developing a new habit to go to God and ask Him for the ability to overcome.

Seek means to try to find, search for; look for, to go to, resort to, to try to get or find out by asking or searching, to request, ask for, to try, attempt, to look for someone or something, to make a search or investigation.[1] We have spent many hours seeking for our favorite addiction so now it's time to seek for the Deliverer from our addiction, who is Jesus. Again, this is an action word—our action. It is an ongoing endeavor which will bring freedom and peace versus prolonged struggle and pain. The temptation to seek other things will be strong but can be resisted. We may seek God for awhile and then revert back to seeking relief from our addiction. We must just keep seeking God. It will get easier.

Knock in Webster's dictionary means to strike a blow or blows with the fist or some hard object, to bump, collide, crash.[2] Knock is a very aggressive word, an action we are to take. We should be knocking on the door of God and His Word instead of knocking on empty doors of sin and addiction. We know we have asked for drugs, money, and fixes; sought how and where to fulfill those cravings; and knocked down doors to get to whatever our fix is. We must do the same thing for freedom by going to a new source—Jesus.

We need to go to God and ask for forgiveness and freedom. Seek Him and His Word, the Bible, for what His truths are and keep knocking at the door of His heart until the door of freedom is swung wide open and the door of addiction is closed for good.

> Therefore, submit to God. Resist the devil and he will flee from you. Draw near to God and He will draw near to you. Cleanse your hands you sinners; and purify your hearts, you double-minded. Lament and mourn and weep! Let your laughter be turned to mourning and your joy to gloom. Humble yourselves in the sight of the Lord, and He will lift you up.
>
> —JAMES 4:7–10, NKJV

Look at the verbs, action words, in the above scriptures: submit, resist, draw near, cleanse, purify, lament, mourn, weep, and humble yourselves. Obeying these instructions is our part. God's part is to then lift us up from the pit that the addictions have thrown us in.

These steps are a starting point, not a formula. A formula or a program will not heal or deliver us but a Person named Jesus can and will. There are good programs like AA and NA, which lead a person to a higher power. I acknowledge this Power as God, the Trinity—Father, Son, and Holy Spirit. Jesus is the Word as stated in John 1:1–4.

First of all we must change what we are submitting to. Our habit has been to submit to the overwhelming urges and desires to bring satisfaction to our flesh through food, alcohol, drugs, sex, improper use of money, or whatever our habit has been. Our new habit will be to submit to God during our times of need and withdrawals. We can do this through prayer by going to God and asking for Him to meet the need we are trying to meet ourselves with our addiction. We submit to His power and authority in our lives instead of the power and authority we have given our sin.

How about the word *resist*? *Resist* means to withstand; oppose; fend off, stand firm against; withstand the action of, to oppose actively; fight, argue or work against, to refuse to cooperate with, submit to; to keep from yielding to, being affected by, or enjoying, to oppose or withstand something; offer resistance.[3] When our desire is strong for whatever is pulling our attentions, we must resist. That sounds so easy but we know it is very difficult. Reread the above definition. Those meanings are powerful, which means the action of resistance is powerful as well.

We can try to resist in our own strength but that gives way to failure too easily. How do we resist? First and foremost, we submit to God. What does that mean? We go to

Him. *God, I confess I am weak and my flesh wants _____ _____ (fill in the blank), but I know that's not really good for me, You are. Help me, Lord, to resist this pull to _____ (fill in the blank), which only leads to heartache.*

Remember, we are in a war and the enemy (your addiction) will not waiver so why should you? If you were held captive in a war camp, would you just give up or would you continue to fight for your freedom and life. This is the same attitude we must have to stand against our addiction. I believe it is a process we must all go through.

What does cleanse your hands mean? My thought is that we cleanse our hands by releasing from our hands to God whatever the addiction is, asking Him to take it. It also definitely means making no provision for the flesh.

> But put on the Lord Jesus Christ, and make no provision for the flesh, to fulfill its lusts.
>
> —ROMANS 13:14, NKJV

This means that whatever your addiction is, get it out of your house and surroundings. That's right, get rid of it. It has to go. If your addiction is junk food, throw it out and refuse to buy more at the store. We can't eat what's not in the house. Is it pornography? Get rid of the magazines, put the computer in a central location where everyone can see, or cancel your computer if you must so you don't have access. If you are tempted to go get a hooker, tell a trusted friend when you are tempted. If it's cigarettes or pot, get rid of the lighters, pipes, papers, and ashtrays. If your addiction is to gossip, find new friends who are not tempted in this area and make known to anyone wanting to gossip to you that you are breaking free from that destructive behavior. Maybe you are into drugs, legal or not; get rid of the paraphernalia, avoid the area where your dealers are, and get rid of their phone numbers.

I can't stress enough the importance of distancing yourself from these distractions and temptations. No, this is not easy but the payoff is huge. Freedom is sweet. Bondage is bitter. This pain and fight will not last forever and it will get easier. Bondage will last forever and only get worse and worse, bringing with it all kinds of devastation. Freedom gives; bondage steals more and more.

Are you not sure you're ready for freedom yet? It's OK to admit. It is scary because we have grown accustomed to our bondage. In a sick sort of way, it's our friend. It has brought us a false sense of comfort to a certain point. Anything new is scary. At least we know where we are and that is where we need to start. This is where asking, seeking, and knocking comes in. We can ask God to give us a desire to be free. We knock on His door and ask Him to come into our heart and situation. We seek His Word to see what He has to say about sin and truth and freedom. He already knows what's in our heart and what we have done and will do.

There is nothing we can do to hide from Him. Be honest. We will know the truth and the truth will set us free. (See John 8:32.) Do you know the truth about yourself and your situation? Start today to seek that answer. How is my addiction affecting me and others? *Please show me, Lord.* Where am I fearful of freedom? Fear of failure is a biggie. Many of us don't want to try again and fail. Confess it as sin and renew your mind with the truth of God's Word. He is our helper and advocate.

"Purify your hearts, you double minded" (James 4:8, NKJV). That sounds mean, doesn't it? How can we purify our hearts and not be double minded? If we are secretly holding on to the desire for our addiction, we are being double minded. We may want to be free but still haven't made the commitment to do whatever it takes to achieve that freedom. We purify our heart by talking to God about this. We ask Him to make us single minded and fixated on Him and His provision of freedom. Again, we have our part but He has to enable and strengthen us to go through the process.

Our addiction is a habit. We are not to be overcome with evil but overcome evil with good (Rom. 12:21). In terms of our habit, we must overcome it with something good. We have spent a lot of time on our addiction and something else will need to occupy that time. To get us through, prayer needs to be the main focus of that time. In my experience, though, something tangible will need to be put in place as well. Examples of overcoming evil with good would be a service project, exercise, getting put-off projects done, resting, reading, or helping someone in need. Even getting a puzzle or word search is a good distraction. A good soldier has weapons and uses them, so this is part of our weaponry being used to face battles when they come.

There have been times when the urges were so strong, I literally had to flee. In other words, I just took off walking and talking to the Lord. If you ask God to show you how to resist temptation, He will.

> No temptation has overtaken you except such as is common to man; but God is faithful, who will not allow you to be tempted beyond what you are able, but with the temptation will also make the way of escape, that you may be able to bear it.
>
> —1 CORINTHIANS 10:13, NKJV

Why do you think that lament, mourn, and weep are listed in James 4:9? I think it's because this is an important step in our freedom. How can we do away with something unless we first hate it? We need to mourn what we have done to ourselves, our families, and to God by giving ourselves over to destructive habits. We need to ask God to show us His heartache over the sin. This doesn't mean He hates us, but He does hate the sin. Sin causes destruction and damage, and His love for us is so great.

If we saw our child or loved one cutting themselves or killing themselves with poison, wouldn't we grieve and mourn over their actions? Every time we succumb to our urge to self-gratify, we are hurting our bodies and minds. We are keeping ourselves from the good plan and future God has for us. His will is for our freedom, not bondage. Go ahead and mourn the death of your addiction, it's OK. Feel gloomy about giving it up? That's OK too. Our laughter and joy will be renewed a hundredfold when we are walking out of our prison cell.

Humble yourselves in the sight of the Lord. I don't know about you, but the word *humble* is not one of my favorite words. God has done a huge work in me concerning pride, yet I still have a long way to go. We are to go to God humbly, by confessing that we can't do this on our own. If we could, we would have been free a long time ago. I can't tell you how many times I have had to go and lie down on my face before God, helpless and asking for His help. Does this make a difference? Absolutely! You may not feel a thing, but God sees our heart. If your child came to you like that, how would you respond? You would give love and comfort and do whatever you could to help. God is the perfect Father and loves taking care of His children.

We have discussed several spiritual aspects to gaining freedom. It's also important that we include some practical steps that need to be taken along the way. I would suggest drinking lots of water to flush the body of toxins from whatever physical abuse it has endured. This is needful for our health as well as giving us a positive action.

Rest is another key. While we are on our journey, it's probable that we will suffer from battle fatigue. I give you permission to rest. That may simply mean going outside to look at the clouds, read a book, or even watch a good movie. Too many times we think we have to be busy, which could also be an addiction. I know it was for me.

We are beginning to take helpful, positive steps to ensure a healthy lifestyle. We have abused our body and hated ourselves because of the addiction, so now it's time to show ourselves love.

> For all the law is fulfilled in one word, even in this: "You shall love your neighbor as yourself."
>
> —GALATIANS 5:14, NKJV

We wouldn't deny our neighbor rest, water, or decent food, so why do we think we can or should treat ourselves badly? We must develop the habit of taking care of our bodies. By making better choices, we are loving ourselves.

We must also talk about laughter because it brings healing.

> A merry heart does good, like medicine, But a broken spirit dries the bones.
>
> —PROVERBS 17:22, NKJV

It may be difficult to find something to laugh about while we are suffering in the flesh but it really is medicine for our souls. Rent a comedy, go watch children play, tell yourself jokes, whatever it takes to encourage yourself and bring joy to your life.

I've said it before in other chapters and will say it again; we have to change our thinking. When our mind begins to think of our addiction, we must immediately bring those thoughts to Jesus, think of something good, and flee! Do not underestimate running away from the temptation, people, thought, or trigger. Speak aloud something positive, such as the reward you are receiving from freedom, a scripture you have learned or are learning, or even a song.

I am proud of your desire to walk in freedom and know that you will succeed. Don't give up! Remember that a fall is not a failure, only another starting place as well as a learning experience. May God bless you, your family and your new life of freedom.

Dear Lord,

I need you to break this cycle of addiction in my life. I have given into this habit for so long that I don't know how to get free from it. Help me to change my thinking, my desires, my mindsets, and my actions. I will obey You the best I can, and when I fail, I will receive Your forgiveness and encouragement to keep asking, knocking, and seeking. I humbly ask You to deliver me, free me, strengthen me, and make me whole. I confess my sin to You and receive Your mercy, grace, and forgiveness as many times as it takes. Thank You that Your love is unfailing and eternal.

In Jesus' name I pray. Amen.

Notes

Chapter 2
Quit Struggling with Your Struggles
1. Steve Edwards, "5 Ways to Keep the Scale Moving," #296 Breaking Through, http://www.beachbody.com/product/newsletters/296.do (accessed April 8, 2009).

Chapter 7
Sick of Repenting
1. M. G. Easton, *Illustrated Bible Dictionary*, 3rd edition (Nashville, TN: Thomas Nelson, 1897). Public domain.
2. Ibid.
3. William P. Young, *The Shack* (Newbury Park, CA: Windblown Media, 2007).

Chapter 8
Help! I've Fallen and I Can't Get Up
1. *Webster's New World College Dictionary*, 4th edition (Cleveland, OH: New World Dictionaries, 1999), s.v. "fool."
2. Ibid., s.v. "folly."

Chapter 10
Addicted to Peoples' Opinions
1. *Webster's New World College Dictionary*, s.v. "disable."
2. Ibid., s.v. "disabled."

Chapter 11
What Does It Take to Be Free?
1. *Webster's New World College Dictionary*, s.v. "seek."
2. Ibid., s.v. "knock."
3. Ibid., s.v. "resist."

To Contact the Author

addictionssuck@yahoo.com

www.addictionssuck.com